SHUFFLE UP
AND DEAL

WORLD
POKER
TOUR™

SHUFFLE  UP AND DEAL

Mike Sexton

 HarperResource

An Imprint of HarperCollins*Publishers*

HarperCollins books may be purchased for educational, business, or sales promotional use. For information please write: Special Markets Department, HarperCollins Publishers Inc., 10 East 53rd Street, New York, NY 10022.

FIRST EDITION

Designed by Sarah Maya Gubkin

Library of Congress Cataloging-in-Publication Data

Sexton, Mike (Michael Richard)
  World poker tour : shuffle up and deal / Mike Sexton.— 1st ed.
    p. cm.
  ISBN 0-06-076251-9
  1. Poker.   2. World poker tour (Television program)
I. World poker tour (Television program)   II. Title.
GV1251.S344 2005
795.412—dc22   2004059752

05   06   07   08   09   DIX/RRD   10   9   8   7   6   5   4   3   2   1

CONTENTS

PREFACE

World Poker Tour: Shuffle Up and Deal is your opportunity to learn how to play No Limit Texas Hold 'Em and use expert tournament strategy to participate in and maybe even become a champion at the first professional sport in the history of televised sports that is open to you.

Mike Sexton, the host of the World Poker Tour and a champion player in his own right, shares his tournament-tested strategies and insights gained from watching the professional players go head-to-head at the WPT final tables. We hope this book will give you enough knowledge and confidence so that when you play your next No Limit Texas Hold 'Em (NLTH) poker tournament or home game, you will have the skills to be the last one with the chips. The WPT invites you to make poker a part of your world.

INTRODUCTION

The Story of the World Poker Tour

by Steve Lipscomb
WPT President and Founder

Blend one dedicated dreamer with one visionary businessman, add a talented staff and two savvy commentators, stir in 16 cameras, mix it up with six aggressive poker players, and what do you get? The hottest new sports show on television!

Wednesday night is poker night across the nation when World Poker Tour *airs on the Travel Channel. The brainchild of Steve Lipscomb, the tour attracts more than 25 million people each season to join in the fun as the world's best poker players duke it out in a gutsy battle of brains, skill, and luck. Wielding chips as their swords, six wily warriors of the green felt jab one another with over-the-top raises and deceptive bluffs in a fight to the finish for mind-boggling prizes often in excess of $1 million.*

Lights, cameras, action, drama—no wonder people love the show. They *vicariously feel the thrill of victory and the agony of defeat. After all, about 80 million Americans play poker at home, on the Internet, in casinos, and even on cruise ships. But entertainment isn't the only value that viewers get from watching the WPT; they also pick up something extra—a doable dream. The dream of appearing on television at the final table and taking down Gus Hansen or Annie Duke in a daring heads-up duel for the million-dollar pot at the end of the poker rainbow. "All I have to do is win one of those $60 satellite seats in a WPT casino or online card room and I'll have a chance." They know it's doable because they've seen players like 22-year-old amateur Richard Grijalva take home over $450,000, placing 3rd at the WPT Championship event at Bellagio last year.*

The champion of doable dreams, Lipscomb laid it all on the table four years ago when he asked Lyle Berman for financial backing. Accepting the challenge, Berman moved in with a monster stack of chips to take the game to a higher level. Together they beat the odds and brought home the trophy.

"You know how to play poker, right?" Mark Hickman asked when he telephoned me back in 1999. Mark and I have been friends since childhood, and he knows that I've been playing poker with the same guys for 10 years in a low-stakes home game.

"I need somebody to direct and produce a documentary for the Discovery Channel. Can you do it?"

"Sure!" I said, since I'd been in the business of making documentaries, though primarily for film. That's how I came to produce my first poker show, *On the Inside of the World Series of Poker.*

When I walked into the world of poker, I'd never heard of Texas Hold 'Em. I had been living in Los Angeles for eight years and had no idea that poker was being played in casinos there. In our home games, we play for fun and recreation, as well as a means to get together to enjoy one another's company—like most people who play the great American card game. Really, I think that I represent the core of the people who we have brought into the World Poker Tour, and I believe that it has been helpful to have someone from the outside coming into it.

Essentially, I *am* our audience. From the beginning, I've always thought that if I could produce a show that I would want to watch, I could reach a very broad audience. In making the documentary for the Discovery Channel, I learned a lot about the poker world. When it aired, the documentary doubled its audience in an hour—not many shows do that—which led me to believe that there was an audience out there for poker on television. From there I went on to other projects on my calendar, producing a couple of shows for Comedy Central and creating a show with the legendary Norman Lear, who created the television classic *All in the Family.*

WRITING A BUSINESS PLAN FOR A POKER LEAGUE

The moment of inception of the WPT was in the ether of my mind's eye, but it wasn't until I asked myself, "How can I make poker into a business?" that the WPT really came alive. In September 2001, I finally had a month's breather, during which I sat down and wrote the initial business plan for the world's first poker league. Looking back with 20-20 hindsight, it's almost weird how I seemed to have amassed over the years the eclectic tools it would take to re-create poker as a televised sports sensation—from the writing to the directing, the producing to the editing and the creating, as well as the business sense. And my background in law proved invaluable.

In 2000, I had pitched poker to all types of networks, but none of them believed that televised poker had any chance of being popular in the United States. No one can be faulted for not sharing the vision of poker on television. Poker had been broadcast since the late 1980s on ESPN, but it was done so poorly that it played in filler time slots at two in the morning and served as a constant reminder that televised poker could never be interesting.

One of the myths that surround *World Poker Tour* is that it's been successful just because we show the players' hole cards, but that's not the whole story. Actually, we shoot with 16 cameras, not 4 as has been done in the past. If you look at the way poker was presented on television in the early days—if you line up one of those shows and one of our shows side by side—you'll find that it's an entirely different experience. I had a very strong sense that if you were able to accomplish two basic things, you had a chance of reinventing poker as a televised sport.

The first prerequisite was that you absolutely had to transform the experience for the viewers and make them feel like they were sitting in a seat at the poker table. All the things that we revolutionized and changed to make poker into a televised spectator sport were aimed at accomplishing that end goal. When you watch our show, we want you to feel like you are sitting in the seat: you're sweating because the other person is about ready to put a million dollars into the pot, and, by golly, it feels like you're putting the million into the pot. That was our prime directive.

The other very important goal was that the show had to play on multiple levels. It had to be something that someone who was a professional poker player, and someone who was an absolute novice at the game, would have enjoyable experiences watching. Not easy to do—but these two things were the holy grails that would allow us to create a show that would appeal to a wide audience.

The reality was that nobody was likely to put money into a venture unless they believed there was a rainbow at the end of that long tunnel. Part of the limited vision beforehand, I think, was viewing poker tournaments as unique, onetime events—and never daring to think big enough to position poker as a sports league on the magnitude of the NBA and the NFL. The notion was to take the premier poker tournaments across the country and roll them up under the banner of the World Poker Tour, to build a brand that could be monetized in many ways for years to come.

LINING UP THE RIGHT PEOPLE

The next task was to assemble a team that was up to the daunting task of creating a new sports league. Enter Robyn Moder, the most talented production maven I knew in the business, and Audrey Kania, a talented business strategist and branding expert with a Disney pedigree. Then I approached Mike Sexton and Linda Johnson, two cornerstones of the poker world and known to most as the ambassadors of poker. "I have something that I think will change poker forever," I told them. "I want you to walk through it and see what you think."

Down in a jungle restaurant in Costa Rica, they sat and read the business plan with me and immediately saw that this was a new gateway for the poker world—one that had a chance of legitimizing the game and the community in a way that had never been seen before. Together we approached Lyle Berman, who was *the* investor in everyone's mind, hoping that he would be interested in backing the concept.

People had been approaching Lyle forever about putting poker on television, but no one had presented a viable way to make televised poker into a business. At that first meeting, he dug out a memo that he had written back in the '80s and had sent to the management of one of the casinos he worked with, saying that he thought it would be terrific if a way could be found to make poker work on television.

We were the first to approach Lyle with the tools and the apparent ability to make that vision a reality. We had a viable business model and a business plan that outlined the vision and the financial requirements. If it was a home run, the WPT would be the NFL/NBA/PGA of poker. It doesn't sound quite as crazy to say that now as it did back then.

I remember walking around in those early days saying, "We're about to launch the PGA of poker," and everyone, including people in the poker community, nodded their heads politely and said, "Yeah, yeah, sure." But in a very short length of time, the WPT started beating television numbers for most sports, including regular-season NBA games.

We went to Lyle's board of directors at Lakes Gaming, and they liked the idea so much that they changed the company's name to Lakes Entertainment. The time line of this business is rather extraordinary. In September 2001 we developed the business plan; in October we approached Lyle for funding; and by February 2002 we were in business. The WPT was and is a charmed project. The people and the results they have achieved are rare and remarkable.

Our next task was to sign up the Who's Who of tournament poker and destination casinos.

It may seem difficult to imagine today, but our charter member casinos had never been approached by anyone to film their poker tournaments. And there is no reason to believe that they would. Our strategy was to make them an offer they couldn't refuse. We guaranteed them that we would broadcast a two-hour show covering their tournament and featuring their casino at least twice. They would get a tremendous amount of exposure, it would cost them very little to participate, and all they really needed to do was agree that they would be exclusive to us long term for televised poker. The key was that we did not want to build this world, create the success, and then let someone come along and steal it out from under us. Believe me, that was critical to the long-term health of our business. Today, all WPT venues are contacted many times a month by people who would like to step in and benefit from the poker meccas we have managed to create together.

The process of approaching these casinos was truly something out of the movies. The first casino to sign with us was Foxwoods, the largest casino in the world. Walking into the Foxwoods conference room, Audrey and I met with literally legions of people sitting around the largest conference table I've ever seen—every vice president and department head was there. All we brought were a flip chart and our passion.

"We're about to launch a new sport," I began. "It will change the poker world, but more important for you, it will promote the heck out of your casino and bring people streaming through your doors." The credibility of Lyle's name went a long way, and the actual story was a good one that led people to believe (1) this was not a big risk; (2) if it hit the bull's-eye, it would be great for them; and (3) we were people to trust. We walked out of the meeting pleased that there seemed to be some interest.

Half an hour later, I got a call on my cell phone from Kathy Raymond. She said they were "in." The relationships we have forged with the best casinos and card rooms in the world have been critical to the success we have had to date and will, I believe, continue to provide long-term benefits to them as well as us.

After Foxwoods signed up, approaching all the other casinos was that much easier. The next to sign was Bellagio, recognized by many to be the center of the high-stakes poker world. Once Doug Dalton stepped in with a commitment from Bellagio, casinos began to feel that they would miss out if they did not sign on. Next was the Commerce Casino in Los Angeles (the largest card room in the world). With these three powerhouses of poker committed to the WPT, the rest fell into place in a relatively short period of time. By the middle of May 2002, we had signed a full contingent of charter member casinos to launch the first WPT season.

ROLLING THE DICE

Understand that there was no proof that poker would work on television—no proof to the point of distraction—and we still had to sell the concept to a network. It was a roll of the dice. *Late Night Poker*, which had been somewhat successful in England, had worked for a little while but had been canceled. The producers had come to the United States trying to sell their show in the U.S. market, but no one would buy it because the show had not convinced anyone that poker would work on television. They hadn't cracked the code.

By June 2002, Robyn, Audrey, and I, along with our talented production team, had already defined our brand image, designed the WPT arena, put together a plan for how to shoot the show, and hired the crew. Filming our first show at Bellagio in Las Vegas was one of those miracle experiences of a lifetime. Our first tournament took place less than four months after we launched the business, an unbelievably fast ramp-up time. If you have been to a *World Poker Tour* taping, you know that it is very difficult to watch the final table and not have one of those wide-eyed, I-can't-believe-it kind of expressions on your face. I will never forget sitting beside Robyn after that first shoot, watching the now-still set and saying, "I can't believe we pulled it off." As with all of the moments in the launch of the WPT, I have been blessed to be surrounded by quality people with extraordinary capabilities—people never seem to flinch when I ask them to do the impossible.

This may sound like the end of the story, but it isn't. We had put things in the can that we thought were meaningful—now we had to figure out how the heck to make it into a show. I had never directed multicamera shoots before, but I knew that I was the only person who knew poker well enough, and understood the television stuff well enough, to be sitting in the director's chair. We had 16 cameras working simultaneously, synched together, to film a seven-hour final table. Now how do you make that into a compelling two-hour show? The next eight months were all about how to do that.

In the meantime, we filmed other tournaments, but the process of literally creating a way that poker could live on television was an eight-month process—it took us that long to get it right, to get a show together. March 30, 2003, was showtime.

SELLING THE SHOW TO THE NETWORKS

It is amazing that once we announced that we had raised millions of dollars and were actually going to broadcast the WPT with or without a dedicated broadcaster, the networks that had not previously been interested in televised poker started calling. The people at the Travel Channel—and particularly Doug DePriest and Steve Cheskin—deserve a lot of credit for the risk they took on the *World Poker Tour*. Without seeing one frame of videotape, they ordered a full season of 13 two-hour episodes and promised a prime-time slot on Wednesday nights. Other networks were willing to air an episode or two to try the show out, but I reminded Lyle of the promise we had made to each other when the business began.

"If we're not willing to spend enough to completely revolutionize what's being done with poker," I had told him in our early discussions, "I don't want to do the show." "And, no matter what, we need to hold out for a regular weekly time slot." The key to our success would be to make poker appointment television—even if that meant we had to start by buying airtime on television. He agreed with both of these major necessities.

A tremendous amount of power goes into motion once you start rolling and getting things done. This charmed WPT project began with a concept in my twisted brain that became a business plan. From that business plan, Audrey Kania, Robyn Moder, Mike Sexton, and Linda Johnson came into the mix. Then on to Lyle Berman and millions of dollars. And then Melissa Grego wrote the first article about us, which ran in *Variety* and was picked up on a wire service. Because of her article, the announcement that Lyle Berman and Steve Lipscomb had formed a joint venture to launch *World Poker Tour* appeared all over the country.

Her article actually gave us something that money can't buy. And that's rare. But she loved the story because it was unique. When that article came out, we got the attention of broadcasters, who started coming to us; usually, most television producers have to beg broadcasters to put them on the air.

The people at the Travel Channel were willing to do what most broadcasters are reticent to do—take a risk on the unknown. They dared to be dealt into a hand when they had no idea what cards would come up. And indeed they hit the jackpot: the WPT literally transformed the network. When it started airing our show, the Travel Channel's prime-time average was 350,000 households watching their programs. In the first season, the WPT consistently reached an audience of 1.2 million households, numbers that were way above anything the Travel Channel had seen before.

The story of the WPT is writhe with poker metaphors. From the very beginning, the WPT has been a series of all-in bets. The opportunities that my team and I passed up to focus on and dedicate our lives to poker were all-in bets for everyone. I felt good that I was able to hire people who are smarter than I am to produce and promote the show. Robyn and Audrey opted to pass up all the other opportunities that came to them and jump onto my crazy idea. Early on, Robyn was the person who made things happen in production, while Audrey created the vision to expand the brand beyond television. They put all their chips on the line in producing the show and making the vision a reality.

Today, 24 million people watch the WPT on television each season. According to the *New York Times*, 50 to 80 million people play poker regularly. We want recreational poker players to come to our show, but we also know that a lot of people who watch the WPT are not poker players. Even people with little or no experience whatsoever at playing poker love our show because of the entertainment value it offers them.

THE IMPACT OF A POWERFUL PRESENTATION

Our intent was to re-create poker as a sport. To accomplish that goal, we had to allow viewers to follow the game. Not only do you see the cards, you see their values and meaning through our graphics.

A lot of emphasis has been put on the lipstick cameras. And it's true that the WPT Cams are a terrific way to make poker interesting on television, because they make you feel like you're in the player's seat. But equally important is our graphics palette, which every other poker show has copied. Part of the artistry inherent in WPT productions is painting the details of the poker action onto a TV screen to give people a vivid picture of what poker is all about.

The WPT graphics are what make our shows watchable so that our audience can follow the action, but the palette is so subtle that many people don't realize how much it adds to the show. Our graphic breakthrough shows you what's happening in a meaningful way so that you can follow the action as it goes around the table and compare it with the community cards. Having the pot size and other information coming up on the screen to let viewers know what's going on had never been done before.

Then we added elements such as player bios so that viewers can actually develop a rooting interest in the players, similar to what was done on the telecasts of the 2004 Olympic Games in Athens.

From the producer's standpoint, the game of poker is incredibly microscopic. We thought that if poker was going to be interesting for people to watch, we had to create a show that captured the microscopic, not the macroscopic. If you look at the macroscopic, poker doesn't appear to be something that people might like to watch. But if you focus—if the camera is on the player's hands as he releases his chips, if you focus on his face as he bets or reacts to someone else at the table—you catch the drama.

If you're there at every microscopic moment, poker becomes a fantastically interesting sport. We brought in Mike Sexton and Vince Van Patten as our commentators, similar to sportscasters at football games. The WPT Cams, the graphics palette that translates the action, and our commentators create live fiction.

"Live fiction" is the term that I coined so that our producers and editors would understand me every time I said, "You just violated the rule of live fiction. If it doesn't feel like it could happen 'live,' you don't play it." The fiction, of course, is that our show is playing live on TV. You see, poker had always been represented previously on TV as a documentary type of show. The WPT changed all of that. Our show plays "live," like a sport that's happening *now*. I think that's a huge deal.

For example, after we had finished filming the day's shoot at the Reno Hilton, we went to the bar and watched the tournament we had filmed previously at the Bicycle Casino, which was airing for the first time on the big screen. A guy sitting near us told his buddies, "You know, they're filming that show here in the casino right now." Like the men at the bar, I think there are a tremendous number of people who think they're watching a live event. And that's as important as any of the other elements in our show.

ADDING COMMENTARY AND COLOR

The other important element of our show is the commentary. Poker commentary in the past was very similar to the experience of going to a nuclear physicists' convention. The "poker speak" was so thick in previous poker shows that most of us could not understand it, got turned off by it, and consequently turned off the program.

We spent a lot of time with our first show, redoing the audio three times in order to make it as simple as it could be. When we began, there was a lot of directing and adapting of the commentators' styles so that their interaction became very conversational, very much like someone was sitting in your living room talking with you about a sport that they love. Now their interaction is natural and effortless.

We want people who know poker to get what they need, to get their "fix," while people who don't know the game can understand from the commentary what is happening at any time. You may not know much about poker, but the commentator just told you that the guy in the blue shirt has been playing poker for five days, and at this given moment he could lose everything because he has no idea that the player wearing the baseball cap just got dealt a huge hand. He's thinking his way through a big decision, beads of sweat start popping out across his brow—this is a crucial moment in the game with huge money on the line. Capturing the inherent drama of this critical moment is what Mike and Vince do for the show.

The networks were accustomed to bringing in people from the sports world to do commentary for their events, people who have a name in the business. We refused all of those requests. Mike is the poker voice. We didn't want a clone of Mike to be his cohost because one of the big problems of previous poker shows was that they had too many poker voices. We brought in Vince because, in addition to having some poker knowledge, he was a smart-enough and savvy-enough entertainer to comprehend that when I said, "I want color," I wanted color, not just two guys sitting there talking about poker.

As we tried to create how poker commentary was supposed to sound, my mantra was this: "I want you guys to have the kind of relationship on camera that entices people to invite you into their living rooms every Wednesday night."

It has always been important for us at *World Poker Tour* to make poker into a sport that everyone believes in and enjoys watching. Without the support of the players and significant fan base, none of this would have happened. The first time we spoke with *Sports Illustrated*, they asked, "Why in the world would we write about poker?" Since then the magazine has published multiple articles about this sports phenomenon that we have created.

From day one, Lyle and I have viewed the WPT as a long-term venture. The whole idea was to reach the point where we have branded poker, established ourselves as leaders in the marketplace, and created something that nobody laughs at when we refer to poker as a sport. Now we have a chance to look toward the future. Remarkably after two and a half short years, the World Poker Tour, LLC became WPT Enterprises, Inc. when we went public in August 2004 and is currently traded on NASDAQ (symbol: WPTE). With ample resources and a bright path, our future includes a strong move into international online gaming market (WPTonline .com), producing other television shows and formats, expanding into consumer products and casino games, and continuing to grow the sport of poker as we maintain our position as the preeminent poker brand in the market.

How big can it become? Really, I can't think of any other sport in North America that is played by as many people as poker. The fact that poker is now being played in places where it never was before—because of the WPT—leads us to believe that we can only grow. We're racing to continually keep up with our own dream.

CHAPTER 1

You Can Become a Winning Poker Player!

If you want to become a winning poker player it will take some time and effort. The truth is that many players don't want to work on their poker game before they play poker for money. They just hope they'll get lucky and catch some cards.

I like to relate poker to golf. Most people don't want to go out to the driving range and beat balls all day long, or practice putting for hours, or blast out of sand traps again and again. They just want to march directly to the first hole, put the tee in the ground, hit the ball, and play golf. They don't want to spend time practicing to improve their skills—it's much more fun to play on the course.

To play poker well, it is essential to work on your game. That includes reading books, watching televised World Poker Tour

(WPT) tournaments on Travel Channel each week, running computer simulations, practicing in games online, and analyzing hands. You can't just walk into a poker room, sit down, and say, "Deal me in!" and hope to get lucky. Occasionally, you will win a few bucks this way, but the key to consistently winning is practice and preparation. As with most things in life, in poker, those who prepare to win will do better than those who don't.

You can start by playing online for free while you're still getting your bearings. With the availability of online poker and the computer simulation programs, books, and educational videos on the market today, you have more opportunities than ever to learn how to become a winning player. One of the most useful tools in improving your game is watching how top players play their hands. Many players watch the WPT DVDs over and over to analyze a player's strategy. Also, WPT's Web site (www.worldpokertour.com) offers tools to help gain insight into players' strategies.

Champion golfer Gary Player once said, "You know, the more I practice, the luckier I get." So true! Like everything in life, the more you work to improve your skills, the better you get at anything you do. Certainly in poker, the better you get at it, the more money you'll win. And that's a good-enough reason for any serious player to want to become a winning player.

Play Just a Little Bit Better Than Your Opponents

You don't have to become the greatest poker player in the world to be a winning player—all you have to do is play a little bit better than a couple of the people you're playing against. You might be only the fourth- or fifth-best player at the table, but you're still a favorite to beat the game because you're better than at least three other people at the table. And that's the key to winning at poker.

Here's a classic poker story that poker legend Doyle Brunson first told years ago that illustrates this point. A reporter had just finished wrapping up an interview with Eric Drache, a tournament director, and moved along to interview Doyle.

"Doyle, I've just finished talking with Eric," the reporter said, "and I understand that he's quite a good seven-card stud player."

"Yeah, he's a great stud player," Doyle answered. "In fact he might be the seventh-best stud player in the world."

"Really? Wow, I didn't realize he was that good!"

"He is good, but Eric has one problem."

"What's that?" the reporter wondered.

"He plays with the top-six stud players every day!"

If you want to become a winner at poker, play at a table where you are a better player than several of your opponents. Game selection—picking the right game to play in—is very important if you want to be successful at poker. You don't have to beat all the players all the time; you just have to beat a few of the players most of the time.

Usually, the higher the limits you play, the better the competition—make no mistake about it. If you are struggling or just breaking even at a limit, try dropping down a notch and playing at a lower limit for a while. One of the most surefire ways to deplete your bankroll is ego. Don't let it hinder you on your way to the winner's circle.

POKER IS ABOUT MAKING CORRECT DECISIONS

Back in the mid-1980s at the Bicycle Casino in Southern California, I attended what I believe was the first-ever poker seminar. The instructor was "Crazy Mike" Caro, who later became known as "the Mad Genius of Poker." The first words out of his mouth were "What is the object of poker?"

"Making money," the first person answered, which certainly sounded correct to me.

"Not a bad answer," Caro said, "but wrong!" (No wonder they call him "Crazy Mike," I thought to myself.)

"Winning the most pots," the next person said.

"No!" Caro answered emphatically. "If winning the most pots is your goal, you should play every pot and raise every time it's your turn. You will likely win the most pots, but you probably won't beat the game."

"Enjoying yourself?" the third person ventured.

"Not a bad answer," Caro repeated, "but wrong!"

Finally, Caro said the magic words: "The object of poker is to make correct decisions." Bingo! Poker is all about making the right decisions. If you make enough correct decisions, you're going to be a winning player. If you make poor decisions, you're going to be a losing player. It's just that simple.

Think of playing poker as running a business. When you own a business, you gather information, make the best decisions you can, and invest your money as wisely as possible, and then you hope to get a good return on your investment. Playing poker is exactly the same way. When you play poker, you gather information, make decisions, invest your money, and hope to get a return on your investment. The difference is that you get to see your results right away in poker, whereas it might take five years before you know whether you've made money on a business investment.

A lot of businessmen are playing poker these days. They enjoy it because poker has everything—the mental challenge of competition, the element of financial risk, and the potential for reward, as well as being a great form of entertainment. And what they really like is that they get to run their own business. In other words, they get to make all the decisions themselves. Should I pass? Should I call? Should I raise? Like successful businesspeople, smart poker players make smart decisions.

CONSTANTLY PAY ATTENTION

People often ask me, "What's the number one thing I can do to become a better poker player?" I always answer with the same two little words: pay attention. You can become a better poker player simply by watching what's going on and learning from your observations, even when you aren't involved in the *pot*.★

Sounds simple, doesn't it? Yet you would be amazed at how many people don't pay attention at the poker table. What happens in most cases is that when they aren't playing a pot—which hap-

★ Terms marked in italics can be found in glossary at the back of the book.

pens about 60 to 80 percent of the time—they start thinking about dinner or watching the overhead TV monitor or whatever, rather than observing how everybody else is playing the hand.

The trick is to remain mentally focused on the game. Your focus can get as blurry as your speech if you drink too much alcohol. Take a close look at the top players at the final table in WPT games and you'll notice that their beverage of choice is a bottle of water. Staying mentally alert also means passing on playing poker when you're tired or when you're worried about things that are going on in the rest of your life.

Your mind is like a computer that is continually whirring away. If you put the wrong numbers into a computer calculation, the computer will spit out the wrong totals. In the business world, that's called GIGO, the abbreviation for "garbage in, garbage out." The same thing happens with your computer brain. Let it wander off course thinking about things that aren't important to the poker game you're playing, and your results will suffer.

But if you constantly pay attention by watching everything that's going on in the game, you can feed your computer mind all the good information that you've gathered and it will process it for you. That's how you come to logical conclusions and make correct decisions. Poker is a thinking person's game, there's no doubt about that.

POKER IS A GAME DESIGNED TO BE PLAYED FOR SOMETHING

I firmly believe that poker should be played for something, no matter how small the stakes. Decisions should matter in poker. And for decisions to matter, there has to be a reward to be won or a penalty to be paid. Take a look at the difference in how people play poker when they're playing for free and when they're paying something to play.

When you're playing for free, as you can do for practice at on-line poker sites, virtually no one throws a hand away. Everybody plays it to the *river*. And why not? You're not punished if you lose.

Since decisions don't really matter when you're playing for

free, what difference does it make whether you win or lose? Basically, you're playing showdown poker. If you lose all your chips, you simply push a button and presto! More chips magically appear in front of you. If you think about it, why would you want to throw a hand away? Folding is no fun. Why not try to catch that *gut-shot straight*? You don't want to sit out a hand and just watch other people play—you want to be involved. And with no penalties attached, why not?

But when you're playing for something—even if it's only a $5 or $10 *buy-in* single-table tournament—you'll see a vast difference in the way you and the other people in your game play poker. Now you're trying to win because you realize that you will be penalized if you lose, a penalty you didn't have to pay when you were playing for free.

In poker you should be rewarded for good decisions and penalized for bad ones. That's the essence of the game. If you make enough correct decisions, you'll be rewarded and come out on the plus side. If you make bad decisions, you'll be penalized and end up on the losing side. That's poker in a nutshell.

LEARN FROM YOUR MISTAKES

Practicing is essential, but make sure you are working with good information. Some people unwittingly practice making the same mistakes over and over again, so they keep getting "better" at them. The key is to learn from your mistakes. You can't afford not to, because mistakes cost money. Recognizing your mistakes and learning from them is the difference between ordinary practice and perfect practice.

One way to overcome your mistakes is to mentally analyze your play during and after each session. Suppose something goes wrong and you lose a pot. Maybe you should have raised to give yourself a better chance of winning the pot instead of just calling, getting *outdrawn* at the river, and losing a pot that you could have won. Or maybe you didn't *get full value* for your hand because you didn't bet when you should have. Ask yourself, "What happened here? Where did I go wrong? How could I have made more money with this hand?"

Another good way to improve your game is to discuss things with another player whose opinion you trust. The old-time road gamblers who traveled together from game to game on the old southern poker circuit spent their driving hours talking about the hands they played. They learned from one another. The next time a tricky situation came up in one of their road games, they had a better handle on how to play the hand. Getting a good player's unbiased opinion about how you played in a specific situation can help you recognize your mistakes and remedy them.

You can also keep a journal. List the type of game, the kinds of players in it, the details of certain hands you played, and how much you won or lost. When you review your notes, you might detect a pattern to your play in the games in which you lost. For example, if you find that most of your losses happened when you were sitting in one of the *blinds*, you can start working on that aspect of your game.

It's okay to lose some hands, but you will lose fewer of them if you continually educate yourself by recognizing and correcting your mistakes. "I think I could've made a better play in that situation," you say. "Had I done this instead of that, I would've won the pot instead of losing it." Learning from your mistakes is key to becoming successful at poker.

EDUCATION PLUS EXPERIENCE
IS THE WINNING TICKET

You can get better at poker in a number of ways. You can watch the players on the WPT to see what they do in critical situations. You can read books. You can talk about hands with players whose opinions you respect. You don't have to reinvent the wheel; you just have to pay attention to who's winning and ask yourself, "What are they doing that's different from what I'm doing?" That's what all poker players should be doing.

When you're playing at a table with a good player who intimidates you, don't sit there trembling with fear—watch him, notice what he's doing, and learn. You'll soon be saying, "Hey, now I see what he's doing. Just look at that raise. Wow, what a great play he made in that spot!" Competing against good players gives you a unique opportunity to become a better player. Take advantage of those opportunities when they come your way.

One of the good things about tournament poker is that seats are randomly assigned. You might find yourself sitting down with some WPT champions the first time you play a tournament. Playing alongside the champion players is one of the greatest thrills in the poker world. You're never going to get to play golf with Tiger Woods or shoot baskets with Michael Jordan. But if you sign up for a poker tournament, you might get to play next to a great poker champion like Doyle Brunson, Daniel Negreanu, Gus Hansen, or T. J. Cloutier. Most of the famous poker champions play tournaments regularly these days because of the huge prize pools, so the chances are good that one of them will be sitting at your table if you play in a big-league tournament. It happens all the time. Be grateful for that opportunity, not intimidated by it.

While practice is essential, you cannot master the game unless you actually start playing against skillful players in real poker games. Not until you get your feet wet in the heat of battle can you become a winning poker player. In the following chapters, I will outline the skills and strategies you will need to pick up so that you, too, can someday make it to the final table in a WPT tournament.

Poker History

• No one knows for sure the true origin of the word "poker." Some believe it comes from the magician's term "hocus-pocus."

• From 1910 to 1931, antigambling legislation was so strict in Nevada that it was illegal to flip a coin for the price of a drink.

• In the third day of a marathon poker game, Hall of Fame player Johnny Moss had a heart attack and was rushed to the emergency room. Six hours later he returned to the game for another two days.

• Richard Nixon financed his first congressional campaign with poker winnings.

• According to the United States Playing Card Company, it was the French who introduced today's standard four suits: diamonds, hearts, spades, and clubs.

• Americans, however, invented the joker.

• When President Harry S. Truman said, "The buck stops here," he was really talking about poker. "Buck" is another word for the *dealer button*.

• During the French Revolution, kings, queens, and jacks were renamed Nature, Liberty, and Virtue.

• In 1911, Attorney General Harold Sigel Webb legalized poker in California by declaring it a game of skill and not chance. Thanks, Harold.

CHAPTER 2

The Basics of No Limit Texas Hold 'Em

No Limit Texas Hold 'Em—it takes a minute to learn and a lifetime to master! If you already know how to play the game, you can skip this section and move right along to the next chapter. But if you've never played or would like a refresher course, here's an explanation of the mechanics and basic strategy of the game that will put you in the driver's seat.

Trust me, folks, No Limit

Hold 'Em is the most exciting poker game in the world. At any time, you can literally win or lose everything in the deal of a hand. That's because in No Limit Texas Hold 'Em, you can bet any amount at any time (that is, you can bet all your chips at one time). You can't do that in poker games that have a set limit on the amount you can bet (called limit games). The element of risk— knowing that you can win it all or lose it all at once—is what sets No Limit Hold 'Em apart from other forms of poker. There's nothing like big-bet poker to get your adrenaline flowing!

Now let's take a look at the basics of how the game is played. Follow along as we go through each of the four betting rounds in No Limit Hold 'Em. You'll get a handle on the game and learn the special language of Hold 'Em. As we say on the World Poker Tour, "*Shuffle up and deal!*"

BETTING ROUND ONE: THE DEAL

The game begins when the dealer deals two cards facedown to each player at the table. These are your *down cards*, also known as *hole cards* or your "hand." Nobody else can see your hand (remember, it's your job to protect your hand), and you can't see the hands of your opponents while you're playing the game. If you're playing at the final table of a WPT tournament, of course, you will get a bird's-eye view of your opponents' cards via the *WPT Cam*—but not until the show airs on television.

When you play poker in home games, one of the players in the game deals the cards, starting with the first person to his left. When you play poker in casinos or online, a house dealer will be provided. The dealer is a specially trained casino employee. He delivers the cards to each player (in a clockwise rotation), like a postman delivering the mail, starting with the first player to the left of the *dealer button*. The *button* (representing the theoretical dealer) is a white disk that the dealer moves with every deal of the cards (the exception being something that's called a "dead" button—which is a method of rotating the button that a number of casinos use to make sure everyone puts in their blinds on every round).

The first player to the left of the button is called the *small blind*. The second player to the left of the button is called the *big blind*. Both of these players must put a mandatory amount of chips into the *pot* before the cards are dealt. Since they have to place *bets* before they have seen their cards, they are betting "in the blind." The purpose of the blind bets is to stimulate the action by building a pot of money to compete for at the start of the round. The big blind must put in one full bet and the small blind usually puts in one-half of a full bet. (For example, if the big blind is $100, the small blind would be $50.)

Start Your Motors: The Action Begins

The first player sitting to the left of the big blind (called being *under the gun* because he has to "shoot" first) begins the first round of betting by "acting" in one of three ways. First, if you like your hole cards, you can *call*. You call by betting an amount of chips equal to the big blind. If you like your hole cards a whole lot or are feeling frisky, you can *raise*. To raise you must bet an amount of chips that is at least twice the size of the big blind—and at the most, all of your chips. And if you are the first player to act and you don't like your hole cards or you don't want to put any money into the pot, you can *fold*. Just slide your cards facedown toward the dealer and you are out of action until the next hand is dealt.

If you aren't the first player to bet—somebody else has acted before it's your turn to act—you can do one of the same three things as above: (1) you can call by matching the size of your opponent's bet, (2) you can raise by at least doubling the amount of chips your opponent has bet, or (3) you can fold.

In No Limit Texas Hold 'Em, a lot of tension and excitement is created when a player raises *all-in*—pushes his or her entire stack of chips into the center. You can go all-in on any hand when it is your turn to act. There is a minimum amount that you must bet to continue playing the hand, but there is no limit on how much you can bet at any one time—up to the amount of chips you have in front of you. That's what makes No Limit Hold 'Em so exciting!

After everybody at the table has had a chance to act on their hands (to call, raise, or fold), the dealer places all their bets into a pile (the pot) in the center of the table. Betting Round One is history. Those who have put an equal amount of money in the pot are still in the hand; those who didn't are out and must wait to play the next hand. Assuming you are still in, you anxiously wait for the dealer to put the first three community cards in the center of the table.

BETTING ROUND TWO: THE FLOP

THE FLOP

Betting Round Two begins when the dealer burns a card (the top card on the deck doesn't play) and then lays three cards faceup in the center of the table. These are *community cards* that you and everybody else at the table can use. The first three community cards are called the *flop* because the dealer flops them over as he or she removes them from the deck.

The betting starts with the first player to the left of the dealer button who is still in action—that is, the first player who did not fold in Betting Round One. If you get to act first, you can do one of two things.

First, you can *check* by opting not to make a bet. You do this by verbally saying, "Check," or by knocking on the table. Note that this doesn't mean you're out of the hand; it simply means that you don't wish to bet at this particular time. (Don't throw your cards away when you check. Hang on to them until someone else bets and then decide what you want to do.)

Second, you can bet. If you bet, you must bet at least the size of the big blind. Of course, since you're playing no limit poker, you can always bet any amount you want to, up to the size of your *stack* (the number of chips you have in front of you).

If the first player checks, the next player to act after him has the same two options. He can check or bet. If nobody bets, the flop is said to be "checked around." In that case, play proceeds to Betting Round Three. But as soon as anybody bets, the players who get to act after the bettor cannot check—they must either call, raise, or fold. And remember, in every round of betting, to continue playing, all players must put an equal amount of money in the pot (the exception being when someone is all-in, meaning that player has all of his or her chips in the pot).

As soon as everybody has acted, the dealer piles up all the bets and puts them in the pot. Round Two is a done deal. The stakes are growing and the pot is getting fatter.

BETTING ROUND THREE: THE TURN

THE FLOP   THE TURN

Betting Round Three begins when the dealer (after burning another card) turns one more community card faceup in alignment with the flop cards. Now you and the other players who are still active in the hand have six cards to select from to make the best five-card poker hand. Count 'em up—you have your two hole cards plus the four cards in the middle.

We call the fourth community card *fourth street* or the *turn* card. You and the players you're competing against realize that there is only one more community card to come. And after you see that one last card, your destiny is sealed.

The betting proceeds the same way it did in Round Two. The dealer rakes all the bets into the pot and prepares to deal the final community card. Warning: you can get knots in your stomach at this point—whether you're trying to catch a card to win or praying that your hand holds up.

BETTING ROUND FOUR: THE RIVER

THE FLOP   THE TURN   THE RIVER

Betting Round Four begins when the dealer (after burning a card) places one final community card, called *fifth street*, faceup next to the turn card. This final card is also called the *river* card. Some players get there with a leaky canoe. It's nice to get there with a battleship, but sometimes a rowboat is enough. It all depends on how your hand stacks up against the opposition or how the last *round of betting* proceeds.

Now you have seven cards (your two down cards and the five community cards) from which to make your best five-card poker hand. You can use just one, or both, of your hole cards to make your best possible hand—and sometimes, you don't have to use either. On rare occasions the community cards (called "the board") are the best possible hand. In that case, everybody who's still in the hand is *playing the board*.

The betting sequence is the same as in Round Three. After each player has acted, the action is said to be "complete" and the dealer brings all the bets into the pot. It's skip-a-heartbeat time as you wait to see if you're going to win all those chips piled up in the middle of the table.

THE SHOWDOWN

PLAYER 1   PLAYER 2

THE SHOWDOWN

In this hand, Player 1 would have taken the pot with two pair (kings and deuces), while Player 2 had one pair (kings) and a busted straight draw.

All the money is in the middle—it's time for the *showdown*! You and your opponents have to turn your hole cards faceup in front of you. Now it's read 'em and weep—or read 'em and reap! (The player who initiated the final betting is obligated to show his or her cards first. If everyone checked, then the player to the left of the dealer button shows down first.) The dealer pushes the pot to the player with the best five-card combination of his or her hole cards and the community cards. It's that simple!

THE DIFFERENCE BETWEEN LIMIT GAMES AND NO LIMIT GAMES

In games with a limit on the amount you can bet, you know in advance how much it will cost to enter each pot. If you are playing $2–$4 Limit Hold 'Em (meaning the small blind is $1 and the big blind is $2), for example, you know that your opening bet must equal the size of the big blind ($2). If you want to open the betting with a raise, you must bet exactly double the size of the big blind ($4). Or if you want to *reraise* someone who has raised in front of you, you must put in exactly as much as him ($4) and then raise it another $2 (for a total of $6). If your opponent has raised to $6, you can reraise to $8, no more and no less. Some casinos have a bet and three raise maximum per betting round; others allow a bet and four raises. Wherever you are playing, ask how many raises are allowed before you start. Putting in the maximum allowed per betting round is called *capping* it.

In games with no limit on the amount you can bet, you are not restricted to betting or raising a predetermined amount of chips. You can open by betting the exact amount of the big blind, or you can open by betting any amount up to the number of chips in your possession. In a $2–$4 No Limit Hold 'Em game, suppose on the second round of betting an opponent bets $12 in front of you. If you want to reraise, you must put in at least $24 to match his bet. But you can reraise more than that if you want to—and you can even bet all your chips if you like (go all-in).

Many players like the structured betting limits in Limit Hold 'Em games, while others prefer not being limited in their betting options. The two games have different characteristics. Players usually play a wider variety of hands and enter more pots in Limit Hold 'Em games. Most people tend to play fewer hands in No Limit Hold 'Em, because all their chips are at risk every time they play a hand. In Limit Hold 'Em games, you will often see several players in each pot (called "multiway" pots). No Limit Hold 'Em pots usually are played one-on-one (*heads-up*) or three-way at the most. In Limit Hold 'Em games, players generally play a lot of hands through the flop, and many hands to the river. Players *see* (call to play) far fewer flops in No Limit Hold 'Em because they often fold to big raises during the pre-flop betting.

No Limit Hold 'Em is the game played at every tournament on the World Poker Tour with the exception of the PartyPoker.com Million, which features Limit Hold 'Em. The PartyPoker.com Million is the largest Limit Hold 'Em tournament in the world.

In contrast to cash games in which you can continue to play by buying more chips when you run out of them, you cannot buy more chips in *freeze-out* tournament games. Players must exit the arena as soon as they have lost all their chips. Thus the winner of a tournament is determined through the process of elimination. The last player with chips—the player who wins all the chips on the table; the king of the hill; the last man standing—is declared the winner and receives the top prize money. If it's a WPT event, that means megabucks, the beautiful WPT trophy, and a day in the sun when the Travel Channel broadcasts the WPT tournament to millions of television viewers on Wednesday night.

THE BASIC PLAY OF A HAND IN NO LIMIT HOLD 'EM

In every poker game you play, your goal is to either win the most chips you can or lose the least chips possible. In No Limit Hold 'Em games, you often are only a hand away from being a big winner—or one away from losing everything. All your chips are at risk every time you play a hand (the exception being if your opponent has fewer chips than you do).

You should always play good "starting" hands (hole cards). Since you usually aren't dealt good starting hands very often, you should be folding most of the hands you are dealt before you even see the flop. Generally speaking, premium starting hands are high pairs—aces, kings, and queens—or an ace-king suited or unsuited. You also can play a few other hands, depending on your *position*— where you are sitting in relation to the big blind or the button.

Your position in the betting sequence plays a big role in which hands you play and how you play them. The closer you are to the big blind, the stronger the hand you need to come into a pot. When you are one of the first players to act (bet, raise, or fold), meaning you are in the *early position*, throw away anything except premium cards. If you are sitting in the middle of the pack ("middle position"), you can play most pairs and two high cards headed by an ace or king. When you are sitting on the button or one seat in front of it, you can add pairs and *suited connectors* to the list. Be very careful about which hands you decide to play when you are in the small blind or big blind. (Remember, you have to act first on every round of betting after the flop, and that is an advantage for your opponent.)

To show you how basic strategy works, let's play a sample hand from start to finish. Suppose the first two players to the left of the big blind fold. You are the next player to act and you have the A♠ K♦, a premium hand. You can just call the amount of the big blind, or you can raise. Usually, you would come into the pot with a raise of about three times the size of the big blind. The players who get to act after you can call the exact amount of your raise, reraise by putting in an amount that is at least equal to the size of your raise, or fold.

Everybody folds until the player sitting one seat to the right of the big blind. He reraises an amount that is double your original bet. Every player sitting between the reraiser and you can call, reraise, or fold. Let's say they all fold.

When the action gets back to you, you can either call by putting in the exact amount of your opponent's reraise, reraise by putting in at least twice the size of his bet, or fold. In this example, you probably would call the amount of the reraise, but you might want to reraise or fold (which most likely would depend on who your opponent was). You will have to act first after the flop, so you will be at a disadvantage. You cannot predict how your opponent intends to play the hand, but your opponent will have the advantage of knowing your betting action, which will help him decide what to do.

Suppose the flop cards are the A♥ 8♣ 3♠. You like this flop because you have flopped the top *pair* and the top *kicker* (the other card in your hand)—aces with a king kicker. Being the first to act, you can bet or check. Usually you would "lead" (make the first bet) by putting in a big bet, but in this case, you might want to check in hopes that your opponent will bet. If you bet and your opponent calls, the dealer will rake all the chips into the pot and proceed to deal fourth street. If he folds, the dealer will put your opponent's cards in the *muck* (the discard pile) and push the pot to you. You've won the hand. (Note: never turn your cards back in to the dealer until he or she has pushed you the pot.)

Let's say that you lead out and bet on the flop and your opponent calls your bet. The dealer turns up the 9♣ on fourth street (the turn). You lead into your opponent with a big bet. This time he doesn't call—he raises all-in. Now you have two options: call the size of his all-in bet or fold. You cannot reraise since he has no more chips.

You realize there's a chance that the 9♣ helped his hand by making two pair—aces and nines, or maybe nines and eights—or giving him a *flush draw* if he has two clubs in the hole, or even a *set* of nines if he has two nines in the hole. Still, you have *top pair* with top kicker, and you have more chips than he has. You call.

Since you are the only two players in the hand and your opponent is all-in, you both turn your cards faceup. Your opponent has the A♦ 9♦. That explains why he didn't raise when you bet on the flop—he has a weak kicker with his ace. And why he went all-in on the turn—he hit his kicker to make two pair. You have only one pair. At this point his hand is better than yours.

The dealer brings all the bets into the pot and proceeds to deal fifth street. The river card is the K♥. Bingo! You've drawn out on the river by making the top two pair. Even though your opponent also has two pair (aces up), your aces and kings are higher than his aces and nines, so you win the hand. The dealer pushes the pot to you. You are a happy camper. You had the best hand before the flop and on the flop, then he had the best hand when he caught a nine on the turn (giving him aces and nines), and, finally, you caught a king at the river (making aces and kings), outdrawing him. How sweet it is!

Now that you know the basics of the game, you can start having the time of your life playing No Limit Hold 'Em, the most exciting poker game on the planet. The strategy tips in the next chapter will help you win at No Limit Texas Hold 'Em in WPT satellite games and tournaments, in home games, at casinos, and on the Internet. As you've heard me say on TV, "May all your cards be live and your pots be monsters!"

WHAT IF?

What if I want to call someone's bet, but I don't have enough chips?
Even if you don't have enough chips to call the full bet, you can still remain in the hand by calling the bet with all of your remaining chips, or going all-in. In that case, you are eligible to win the amount of chips you have in the pot plus an equal amount of chips from your opponent.

What if there are three players in the pot on the flop, but one of them doesn't have enough chips to call a bet on the turn or the river?

The player with insufficient chips to call the amount of the bet can remain in the hand by calling the bet with all the chips in his or her possession. In that case, the all-in player's bet is put in the main pot, along with a matching amount from the other two players in the pot. Then the dealer creates a *side pot* composed of the extra amount of chips wagered by the other two players. At the showdown, the all-in player is only eligible to win the main pot. The other two players are eligible to win both pots.

What if another player and I have the same hand at the showdown?

If you and your opponent have the same hand at the showdown, you each will receive one-half of the chips in the pot. For example, suppose you have J-10 and your opponent has Q-10. The board is showing A-K-Q-J-6. Taking the best five-card hand, you both have an *ace-high* straight, so each of you wins one-half the total number of chips in the pot.

What if one player raises and another player reraises; how much money do I have to put in the pot to continue playing the hand?

You must put in the amount of the raise plus the amount of the reraise to continue playing your hand. For example, if the first player raises to $100 and the second player reraises to $300, you must put in $300 to remain in the hand. The player who put in $100 would have to add $200 to match the reraise and stay in the game.

What if I'm playing in a cash game and run out of chips?

When you go broke in a cash game, you may buy more chips and continue playing in the game. However, you can-

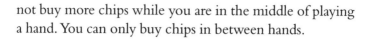

not buy more chips while you are in the middle of playing a hand. You can only buy chips in between hands.

What if I'm playing in a tournament and lose all my chips?

When you go broke in a tournament game, you must vacate your seat and leave the table. You are out of action for the remainder of the tournament.

What if two players go out of a tournament on the same hand at the final table?

When two players get busted on the same hand at any of the "money" tables in a tournament, including the final table, the player who started the hand with the most chips wins the higher of the two payouts. For example, if the fifth-place prize money is $7,500 and the sixth-place prize money is $5,000, the player who started the hand with the most chips is deemed the fifth-place finisher, and the other player who went out in the same hand is the sixth-place finisher.

What if I want to play in a tournament but don't have enough money for the buy-in?

Welcome to the satellite system! You can play a satellite to try to win your tournament entry for a fraction of what it would cost you to ante up the buy-in for the main tournament. Or you might buy in to a cash game and use your winnings for your tournament buy-in. Some players offer shares of their tournament action in exchange for part or all of the tournament buy-in, although getting backers usually requires that you have a track record in tournament play. For a list of WPT Satellite tournaments go to www .worldpokertour.com.

CHAPTER 3

What Separates the Winners from the Losers?

As Kenny Rogers sang in his famous lyric, "You got to know when to hold 'em, know when to fold 'em." That's what separates winners from losers in poker. But the real question is "How do you know when to hold 'em and when to fold 'em?" This is where experience becomes a major factor in your success at the table. The more you play, the better you will become at getting a feel for the game. Now let's take a look at some of the other characteristics that winners possess and losers lack.

Poker is all about betting. For example, if you and I sat down to-gether and played 5,000 hands of poker and neither of us ever made a bet, theoretically you would win 2,500 hands and I would win 2,500 hands. From this example, you can easily see that betting is what the game is all about. It's what determines who wins and who loses. The bottom line is that you must know when to bet and when not to bet—in other words, when to hold 'em and when to fold 'em.

Simply stated, the difference between winners and losers in poker is that winners bet most of the time and losers call most of the time. To be successful at poker, especially No Limit Hold 'Em, you need to be an aggressive player. This doesn't mean that you shouldn't play solid poker, or sometimes play a little bit on the tight side. It simply means that when you do play a pot, you must be ag-gressive. You must take the lead in the pot, be the one who is forc-ing the action.

Why is betting so important? The simplest way I know how to explain it is through the following example. Suppose you're at the river and it's your turn to act. If you bet, you have two ways to win the pot: (1) you can win it with the best hand; and (2) you can bet, your opponent folds, and you win the pot. Now suppose you're at the river and you just call. You only have one way to win the pot: you must have the best hand. Just in terms of simple math, you can see that betting is 2-to-1 better than calling. Understanding this simple concept will greatly improve your results.

To illustrate the downfall of continuous calling, we have an old saying in poker that goes like this: "If you can't beat a 'calling station,' you can't beat anybody." A calling station is someone who's always calling—they aren't betting, they aren't raising, they're just checking and calling. They are the easiest opponents to beat in poker. If you can't beat these players, you need to take up golf or tennis or croquet; poker's not your game.

Calling stations are dream opponents. They are nonthreatening players against whom you can play with confidence and make value bets (bets you make with marginal hands). You figure that you can safely bet a marginal hand into Joe, for example, since you've never seen him raise or reraise anybody else at the table. All he's ever done in previous hands is call, so you know you're not in much danger of having Joe force you out of the pot with an *over-the-top* raise. He's a calling station, a player who is too timid to do anything except fold or call. How much sweeter can it get?

WINNERS CAN PUT THEIR OPPONENTS ON A HAND

The difference between great players and good players is that great players can *put their opponents on a hand* better than others. That is, they know how to make educated guesses as to the value of their opponents' cards. Once you can put an opponent on a hand, you are going to be more successful than the Average Joes or Janes you're playing against.

You get better at this important skill by practicing it during every single hand, even when you aren't playing the hand. "What does John have this time?" you ask yourself, along with questions such as "Why did he bet?" "And why did he bet that amount?" "Why is he checking now?" "Why did he call when his opponent bet?" "Why did he *check-raise* in that spot?" Pretty soon you'll be able to figure out if he has a hand or if he's on a *draw* trying to make a *flush* or a *straight*.

You'd like to figure things out as early in the hand as possible. Certainly by the time you get to the river, you should be able to sort out your opponent's hand fairly correctly just by paying attention and analyzing his or her *actions*. Learning to put your opponent on a hand is a skill that definitely will improve your game and make you a better poker player, pure and simple.

WINNERS HAVE A METHOD TO THEIR MADNESS

You've probably watched the World Poker Tour and seen Gus Hansen and Daniel Negreanu at the championship table playing very aggressively, sometimes staying in pots with marginal hands.

Most poker books say that you need patience and discipline to win at poker, and that you're only supposed to play good hands such as aces, kings, or ace-king. So it's probably hard to understand why these top players are playing the way they do. "How can these guys play a 9-3 or a 10-6 and raise with these kinds of hands?" you wonder. "What's going on here? And why do they win with them? When I try to do that, I lose my money."

There is a method to their madness. They realize that when you're playing against only five opponents at the final table, it's hard to pick up a big hand. They also understand that in No Limit Hold 'Em, you don't need a big hand to win a pot. You don't necessarily even need the best hand to win the pot. The top players win a lot of pots simply by being the aggressor and putting in a bet.

In addition to their betting skills, the best players know how to get away from a hand. By that I mean they'll throw a hand away in a situation where an average player will continue to call to the river, losing bet after bet hoping to get lucky and hit that *straight draw* or something similar. It's okay to be aggressive and try to attack and take the lead, but good players can sense who's going to call them down, when to get away from a hand, and when they can take the pot away from an opponent by simply continuing to bet. That's a fine skill that only the better players have.

WINNERS DON'T CHASE

Winning players are able to fold a hand when they know they're beaten. They don't *chase pots.* When players chase a pot, they call with the worst hand hoping to get lucky and draw a card that will win the pot for them. Yes, they may win some hands that way, but over the course of time they're going to be losing players. Folding is the antidote to chasing.

There is a saying that goes "There are two things that don't last—dogs that chase cars and pros that putt for pars." Poker players who continue to chase don't last, either. One of your goals in poker should be to put your money in the pot when you have the best hand. Let the others chase you; let them call your bets and try to outdraw your good hands. They may get lucky against you sometimes, but they will eventually lose all their money, there's no question about it. If you get your money in with the best hand most of the time, you're going to be a successful poker player.

WINNERS MAKE CORRECT DECISIONS

Poker is all about making correct decisions. During the course of one hand, one pot, let alone the course of an entire evening or a whole tournament, you are faced with making multiple decisions. On every round of action, you must make decisions about whether to check, whether to bet, whether to raise, whether to fold. And if you're going to bet, how much should you bet? If you're going to raise, how much should you raise? You're the boss in making these decisions.

It's your company; you're the CFO. Your job is to run the company in a profitable way. The first decision you have to make—when to hold 'em and when to fold 'em—is the key to success at poker. For people who are relatively new to the game, my recommendation is to just play solid poker rather than trying to make any fancy types of plays. Wait for good starting hands and play them straightforwardly.

Don't try to be creative and play marginal hands such as the 9♥ 6♥. Why? Because at the beginning of your poker career, you don't have enough knowledge and skill to decide what to do with these hands after the flop comes out. On the flop, you will be faced with a whole new set of decisions. Suppose the flop comes J-8-6 offsuit, for example, giving you a pair of sixes (*bottom pair*). "What do I do now?" you ask yourself. If you are new to the game, you can avoid this type of confusion by limiting the number of hands you play until your skills improve.

The great thing about poker is that the more experience you get, the better you are able to make correct decisions. And the better your decision-making skills, the more you can widen your starting-hand requirements because you understand more about how to play after the flop. Go from one step to the next in a logical progression. We all learned to walk before we learned to run. The same thing goes for poker.

WINNERS KNOW WHEN TO CHANGE GEARS

Being able to *change gears* is a key to being successful at poker, especially when you're playing No Limit Hold 'Em. Changing gears means that you change your tempo of play, going from tight to loose and vice versa. You have to play tight poker in certain situations and then change to a faster gear by playing aggressively on other occasions. As Howard Lederer, "the Professor of Poker," says on the *WTP Poker Primer* DVD, included in this book, you always need to be looking for opportunities to play beyond the rules, as this is when you can make the most money.

Two types of players who don't change gears are the "programmed" player (*tight player*) and the "speed" player (*loose* or action *player*). The programmed player cannot freely move from playing tight poker to aggressive poker. Basically, he's a tight player who raises with big hands only. If he decides to gamble, it's usually with a hand such as the 9♣ 8♣ or the J♥ 10♥—and he's going to call instead of raise. Therefore, whenever he calls, you can put him on a hand like that right away. You know that he probably has suited connectors and just wants to see the flop. If he had a big hand, he would have raised.

A programmed player is predictable. Because he plays the same way all the time, he is one of the easiest opponents to play against at the poker table. When programmed players raise before the flop, you know they have a big hand. If you don't have a premium hand, you're better off just stepping away.

Many speed players don't know when to put on the brakes. They don't change gears and continue to lead at too many pots with marginal hands. These overly aggressive players are always in high gear and never slow down. They don't know when to play tight and just sit on their chips to preserve their stack when perhaps they should.

The great players all know how to change gears. They know when it's time to change from a tight strategy to a loose strategy and when to go back to a tight strategy. Being able to vary your style of play and keep your opponents guessing is what separates average players from great players. When you change gears, you make it tough for your opponents to put you on a hand. The strongest asset a player can have is keeping his opponents befuddled about what his hole cards are. "What's he got in the hole?" becomes a pure guessing game that makes it hard for your opponents to figure out how you're going to play a hand.

Certainly if a player comes into every pot—which happens a lot in loose, low-limit games—you're not going to be able to put him on a hand. He's playing every hand, so how can you figure out what he has? But if someone only plays a hand every two hours, you know he's going to have a solid hand, probably aces or kings, when he comes into a pot. To be successful, you need to play somewhere between these two modes.

WINNERS KNOW WHEN TO FOLD

The most financially rewarding play in poker is the fold. Don't be ashamed to fold your hand; instead, take pride in being disciplined enough to fold when you should. A bet saved is a bet earned, as we say in poker. Especially don't be ashamed to fold when you already have some money in the pot. Understand that once you've put money into the pot, it's not your money any longer—it belongs to the pot.

If it seems proper in your mind to not put bad money after good money in the pot, get out of the pot. Forget about the chips you've already put into it. Don't try to get lucky and outdraw your opponent so that you can win those chips back—get away from the hand.

When you put your first money in the pot, you put it in because you think you have the best hand. But things don't always turn out that way. For example, suppose you have the A♠ K♠. The flop comes 10♦ 9♦ 8♦. Your opponent leads out and bets. Your A-K suited is virtually worthless at this point. You shouldn't put any more money in the pot, even if you think that you might win it if you catch an ace. But some players go ahead and play in this type of situation instead of folding. They chase good money with bad money.

Why do they do it? Some people have a mental block that says,

"I've got too many chips in the pot and I've gotta defend them!" Other players have the misguided notion in the back of their minds that their opponents are always trying to steal the pot from them. "Somebody's trying to bluff me out of this pot," they think, "but they're not going to get away with it this time!" They don't want to be embarrassed by getting bluffed out of the money. We call this type of player the "sheriff," poker slang for a player who always calls at the river. "Well, I know you've got me beat, but I'm going to call you anyway," he says as he throws his chips in the pot. You hear it all the time. "That guy sleeps good at night," as we say, because he never has to wonder about what his opponents had. He pays them off every single time. On the other hand, his bankroll is depleting every day.

You don't want to be a calling station at the poker table, but certainly there are times, even in No Limit Hold 'Em, when you do want to check and call your opponent. For example, you may have put the pieces of the puzzle together and believe that your opponent is on a flush draw. You have the top pair or the second-best pair. You've been betting the hand all the way and he's been calling. Now you're at the river. Although you think you have the best hand, if you have put your opponent on a draw, the proper tactic is to check to give him a chance to *bluff* his money at you. If you're right and he has no hand, he's likely to bet to try to win the pot. By checking and then calling, you can earn more money for your hand. However, if you bet at the river, he's probably going to throw his hand away and you won't make any more money. In this situation it is proper to check-call if you think your opponent was on a draw and might bluff at the pot.

You also can use this winning tactic against a very aggressive player. If you know that every time you check your speed opponent is going to bet, why not just check with a good hand? You don't have to bet—let him take the lead. In these situations you'll make more money checking and calling. In poker slang, we call this play "walking the dog."

Another key to success in poker is remaining patient. You hear this advice all the time, but it's a lot easier to preach it than practice it. When you're dealt hand after hand with nothing but junk cards, eventually you begin to lose your patience. Suddenly a K–10 suited looks like two aces, and you say to yourself, "This is the best hand I've seen in an hour. I'm gonna play it!" Don't start playing weak cards in the hope of catching a flop and getting lucky. Folding until you start catching some good cards is a better option.

Winners don't get upset (steam) and play recklessly (go *on tilt*) after losing with a good hand to someone who outdrew them with a worse hand (take a *bad beat*). Patient players don't steam or go on tilt when they take a bad beat or lose a pot. *Steaming* or going on tilt simply means playing bad poker at a certain time in the game.

You can also go on tilt when you realize that you lost because you made a bad play. When you take a bad beat at poker, you might have just been unlucky, or you may conclude that you lost the pot because you played badly. Maybe you didn't bet or raise when you should have, or perhaps you bet when you should have passed.

No matter how your losses come about, you have to maintain your composure at the poker table. You cannot control luck; nobody can. You can, however, control your emotions and how you react to adversity. In golf, if you hit a shot out of bounds, you must put it behind you and forget about it. In poker, if you make a bad play, you must do the same thing.

The late Johnny Moss, the legendary three-time World Champion of Poker, gave me some sound advice years ago. "All you can do in No Limit Hold 'Em is get your money in with the best hand," he said. "You can't control how the cards come out, but if you get your money in 'good,' you'll get the money."

You cannot control the cards you're dealt at the poker table, but you can control your actions—and you absolutely have to control your emotions. A surefire way to deplete your bankroll in poker is to lose your patience and steam or go on tilt. You'll see it happen to even the greatest, most respected poker players at times. Sometimes the best poker game to sit down in is the one where they're playing, steaming, and throwing their money away trying to win it back. They're throwing a party, as we say in poker slang, so why not join in the fun?

WINNERS KNOW HOW TO HANDLE ADVERSITY

Knowing how to handle adversity will help you become a better poker player, that's all there is to it. You've probably seen a pro golfer miss a two-foot putt. He has to put that shot behind him if he wants to continue to play well for the rest of the round. He knows that if he lets it prey on his mind, it's going to affect his results. The same type of adversity happens to poker players. To get past it, you have to tell yourself, "It's over, it's history, forget about it, move forward."

You don't want to let your opponents know that you're upset about anything because they will take advantage of you. They know when you're steaming or going on tilt, and they will play against you accordingly. They'll call you with a marginal hand, one with which they might not otherwise have called if you weren't steaming. You should do the same to them.

Professionals who make their living playing poker know how to get past bad beats and get on with the game—even when they lose with aces in the hole. At the final table of the WPT Season 1 World Poker Finals at Foxwoods Casino, Layne Flack and Phil Ivey had been seesawing between first and second place in the chip lead with Howard Lederer trailing them in the middle of the pack. "I try to take things one hand at a time," Howard told Shana Hiatt, one of the hosts of *World Poker Tour*, in a color interview. But this story isn't about how Howard handles adversity—he's always cool as a cucumber. It's about Layne.

In a key hand that helped Howard move up the money ladder, he raised the pot $12,000 with the K♠ J♦. Layne just called the raise with the A♦ A♥ in the hole, a savvy move that good players sometimes make. He was hoping to *trap* Howard later in the hand and win a big pot. Layne's plan backfired when the flop came K♦ 3♣ J♠. Howard checked and Layne bet $12,000. Howard raised to

$45,000. Layne reraised by pushing his entire stack of chips into the pot. Howard immediately called by going all-in with his two pair, kings and jacks. Now Layne had to catch an ace on either the turn or the river or pair one of the offcards to win the huge pot. It didn't happen.

Getting aces cracked is a brutal beat. Some players would have lost their composure and steamed away a lot of chips as the result. Not Layne. As Howard raked in a big chunk of his chips, Layne literally never blinked an eye, never flinched, never said a word. Showing some class, he let the horrendous beat slide away like water off a duck's back. Layne went on to finish the tournament in second place. Howard won it.

Learn to handle adversity at the poker table and you'll find yourself handling more chips at the end of each session.

WINNERS ARE NOT SUPERSTITIOUS

In my opinion, you're better off not being superstitious at the poker table. "Oh, no, that's my unlucky dealer!" I've heard so many players say when a new dealer comes into the box. They have a negative concept in their mind before the dealer has dealt a single hand. When I play poker, I don't really pay much attention to who is in the box; that way I don't even know who dealt me a bad beat.

Dealers have come up to me and said, "Mike, I'm so sorry I dealt you that bad beat yesterday." And I'll answer, "Was that you? I didn't even know it. Don't worry about it." I tend to not look at the dealer because I don't ever want to think that a dealer is unlucky for me. I think you're better off to just focus on the game and not pay any attention to who's dealing.

Some players even believe that certain seats are unlucky for them. The number one seat comes open in a game, for example, and the guy who comes in to fill it moans, "Oh, no, that's my unlucky seat!" Automatically, he's hexed in his mind before he starts playing. When you play poker, you're better off not getting into things such as which seat is unlucky for you or which dealer has put bad beats on you.

You should never blame the dealer for your bad luck. Simply think of the dealer as the postman who delivers the mail. You don't blame the postal carrier when he brings you bills. You don't take those bills and throw them back in his face. Don't take your frustration out on the dealer.

WINNERS KEEP THEIR THOUGHTS TO THEMSELVES

If I wrote a list of things you shouldn't do at the poker table, criticizing your opponents would be number one. Even if an opponent plays a hand badly, recognize that he has the right to play poker however he wants without being verbally blasted by someone at the table. It's his money and his cards, and he can play them like he wants without being publicly scrutinized.

Some so-called professional players say, "How could you have played that hand? What an idiot! You're going to go broke for sure." Nothing is more frustrating to me when I'm playing poker than for somebody to criticize another player and make him feel bad about his game. One of two things is going to happen: you'll convince him that he's playing very badly and he'll start playing better; or he will decide not to take any more flak, cash in his chips, and leave the game. Either way, the table loses.

I like what Bobby Hoff, one of the original Texas road gamblers and a bona fide great No Limit Hold 'Em player, said in a *Card Player* magazine interview with Dana Smith: "Ambience is what we're selling at the poker table. A lot of people just come to play. If they would honestly admit it to themselves, they would say, 'Well, I can't really win, but I love to play poker. I like the company and it's fun.' But rude players ruin it for them, they ruin it for everybody. And as their 'business partner,' I object! When you mistreat players in a game, they freeze up. They're afraid to play, to make a mistake because somebody's going to get mad. On the other hand, when everybody's laughing and having a good time, the game stays good. Business is good." Certainly there is no advantage to criticizing a poker player at the table. All it does is create a bad atmosphere and cost you money.

In summary, winners are savvy players at the poker table. They are bettors who can accurately put their opponents on hands. They know when to hold 'em and when to fold 'em. They fold instead of chasing pots. Winners have a game plan, they make good decisions, and they know when to vary their style of play.

Winners also possess certain character traits that separate them from losers. They are patient players who handle setbacks calmly. Winners are not superstitious, and they never criticize others at the table.

Now that we've covered the big picture of what winners do—and losers don't do—when they're playing poker, let's focus in on specific No Limit Texas Hold 'Em strategies you can use to become a winner.

Poker Quotes

- "Well, tomorrow's another day"—John Hennigan, after reportedly losing more than a million dollars on a poker game.

- "Mr. Moss, I have to let you go."—Nick "the Greek" Dandalos, announcing an end to his 1949 poker marathon against Johnny Moss. (Legend has it Dandalos lost nearly $3 million to Moss during the five months they played heads-up.)

- "The commonest mistake in history is underestimating your opponent; happens at the poker table all the time."—General David Shoup, 22nd commandant of the Marine Corps.

- "It can be argued that man's instinct to gamble is the only reason he is still not a monkey up in the trees."—Mario Puzo, *Inside Las Vegas.*

- "I once played poker with Tarot cards. I got a full house and four people died."—Steven Wright, comedian.

- "Why, I have known clergymen who did not know . . . the meaning of a 'flush.' It is enough to make one ashamed of one's species."—Mark Twain.

- "I never go looking for a sucker. I look for a champion and make a sucker out of him."—Amarillo Slim Preston.

- "People think mastering the skill is the hard part, but they're wrong. The trick to poker is mastering the luck."—Jesse May, *Shut Up and Deal.*

- "Play to win, or don't bother."—Doc Holliday, in Bruce Olds's *Bucking the Tiger.*

CHAPTER 4

Winning Strategies for
No Limit Texas Hold 'Em

No Limit Texas Hold 'Em is called the Cadillac of poker. Considering the fabulous amounts of money you can win in *World Poker Tour* No Limit Hold 'Em tournaments, that's even truer today than it was years ago when Doyle Brunson first said it. And as we say on the WPT, No Limit Hold 'Em takes a minute to learn and a lifetime to master.

Many of the players who have made it to the final table of WPT tournaments are masters of the game who've spent a lifetime learning the tricks of the trade, so to speak. Others are talented novices having the time of their lives. Whether a proven champion or an accomplished new player, you can be sure that all the players who've made it to the winner's circle have worked hard to get there. They've set certain goals, and, come rain or shine, they've had enough staying power to keep driving forward on the road to success.

If you want to make it to the championship table, you'll get there a lot faster if you set some goals and make a game plan. Like they say in motivational books and seminars, plan your work and work your plan. Since you're reading this book, I know you've already taken the first step. Now I suggest that you use one other method of learning that will help you with your game plan.

Use some of the best poker players in the world as your mentors. "But I don't know any of them," you say. You don't have to know them personally; you can learn by following their example. Try emulating some of their personal traits and doing the things you see them do on our WPT broadcasts. You'll see pros and amateurs alike putting into action the No Limit Hold 'Em strategies outlined in this chapter, and using their unique personal qualities to outwit their opponents. Let me show you what I mean.

You've heard me say that poker is a thinking person's game. Watch Howard Lederer and Phil Ivey use their analytical ability throughout the play of a hand. They think through every move like a chess master. Like Howard and Phil, analyze before you act. Take your time when you're faced with a critical decision—you don't have to act in the blink of an eye. One of the biggest mistakes a player can make is acting too early.

In my opinion, you have to be a risk taker to be successful at anything new. What better model than Gus Hansen, the most successful player on the WPT circuit. Aggressive players like Gus, Layne Flack, and Antonio Esfandiari are willing to lay it all on the line without fear of losing. To do that, you have to feel confident in your ability. Daniel Negreanu is the epitome of "relaxed" confidence. He's friendly and relaxed at the poker table, yet he moves his chips with confidence.

I've never met anybody in poker, in golf, or in any other sport who didn't have the one trait that may be the most important foundation of success—perseverance. Doyle Brunson, the greatest living legend in the poker world today, has stuck it out through thick and thin. He's been robbed at gunpoint, taken unbelievable beats, and went broke time and again early in his career. Yet through all the hard knocks of a 50-year career in poker, he has persevered to reach the highest pinnacle of success.

I'd like to see you join Doyle and other world-class players at the championship table of a WPT tournament. Work on perfecting the strategies in this chapter and use the great players for inspiration, and you'll get there faster than you ever thought possible.

SELECT YOUR STARTING HANDS CAREFULLY

Be selective about the hands you play in No Limit Hold 'Em, but be aggressive when you play them. Enter the pot with good starting hands—big pairs, two big cards, or middle pairs—and don't be afraid to play your hand from the flop to the finish when you get quality cards and hit the flop.

If you are an inexperienced player, you cannot be successful by playing a lot of pots. You simply have to fold a lot of hands in No Limit Hold 'Em. Don't get cute with hands like A-3 offsuit, for example, and try to impress everybody by gambling with them. Even if you hit an ace on the flop, you could be headed for trouble because your opponent could easily have an ace with a bigger kicker.

Here's some good advice for most new players: unless you start with a big pair, the flop needs to hit your hand for you to justify playing it after the flop. "Fit or fold," a maxim coined by Dana Smith, should be your guideline. It means that your down cards need to mesh with the flop in some way. If the flop doesn't fit your hand, you should fold. For example, suppose you have a K-Q and the flop comes K-6-2. You've hit top pair on the flop. And if it comes J-10-9, you've really hit it! On the other hand, if the flop comes 8-7-6, you're a mile away from it, so you should fold if somebody bets into you.

You're better off playing premium cards, of course, but you also can play a few other hands such as *middle suited connectors* or small pairs in the right situations. Many players like to play suited connectors, cards such as 9♣ 8♣ or 7♥ 6♥. I think it's okay to see a flop with them, even if you're a new player, if you only have to call a small bet before the flop. Your reason for playing these types of hands is that they have the potential to win a lot of money from your opponents if you hit the flop. Of course, aggressive players like Daniel Negreanu call the 10♦ 6♦ (connecting cards with the widest gap possible) suited connectors because they like to play a lot of pots!

If no one has raised in front of you, you can call to see the flop with a small pair in the hope of flopping a set (three of a kind). Small pairs are easy to play: if you don't flop *trips*, you simply abandon ship if someone bets the flop.

Middle pairs are much tougher to play. If you flop a set, that's great. But suppose you have a pair of eights and the flop comes something like J-7-3. Whether your opponent bets first and now it's your turn to act, or you bet first and she calls, you should be thinking, "Houston, we have a problem!" In the play of these types of hands, your decision-making skill and instincts are vital. These are the kinds of situations in which it really pays to know your opponents.

Many times, your decisions about what to do depend on who you're playing the pot against.

PAY ATTENTION TO YOUR POSITION AT THE TABLE

Your position is very important in No Limit Texas Hold 'Em. Your position is where you are sitting in relation to the blinds and the button. It is where you are located in the betting sequence. When you are playing in a 10-handed game and are sitting in the first or second seat to the left of the blinds, you are in early position. If you are sitting in the third, fourth, or fifth seat to the left of the blinds, you're in middle position. If you're *on the button* or one or two seats to the right of it, you're in *late position*.

Good players usually determine which hands they play, as well as how they play them, according to their position at the table. For example, they usually will play only the best hands under the gun (the first seat to the left of the big blind), but they might play middle connectors and small pairs when they are in late position.

The earlier your position, the stronger your hole cards should be. The later your position, the more types of hands you can safely play. The reason for being more cautious about the hands you play "up front" (in early position) is that everybody else gets to act after you act. They know how you're playing the hand, but you don't know how they're going to play their hands. They have more information than you do, so they have the advantage over you.

Here's an illustration to demonstrate why being in favorable position is so important. Suppose you are under the gun with two 10s. It's a nice hand, so you enter the pot by raising. Now, the player behind you picks up two queens and reraises, another player with A-K calls, and someone in late position goes all-in with two aces. You recognize that your two 10s are not good anymore, so you fold when the action gets back to you. Notice the difference if you are on the button with those two 10s (instead of being the first to act with them). The player with queens raises, the player with the A-K most likely reraises, and the player with two aces goes all-in. Because you are on the button and have the benefit of seeing all this action, it's pretty easy to now fold the 10s. The point is that when you were in early position with the 10s, you lost money with them, and when you were in late position, you didn't.

You also should pay attention to the types of players who get to act after you. Are they aggressive or passive? If you come into the pot with a raise from early position and an aggressive player is sitting *behind* you—he's sitting in a later position than you—you know he might reraise. Therefore, you want to start with a strong hand that you can "stand a raise" with (defend against a raise). But if only passive players are sitting behind you when you come into the pot with a raise, you know the chances are good that they will just call or fold with anything less than aces or kings. This is one reason why my next topic—knowing your opponents—is key to your success at No Limit Hold 'Em.

OBSERVE HOW YOUR OPPONENTS PLAY

The more you learn about how your opponents play, the better able you are to beat them. If you've been sitting at a table for 30 minutes paying close attention to the game—and I know you are because that's step one of your educational process in poker—you should be able to determine your opponents' usual style of play.

You should be paying attention during every hand so that, at the very least, you know who is a tight player and who is a loose player, especially if it's the first time you've ever played with them. Observe their betting patterns: How often do they play a hand? Do they usually raise when they come into a pot? Do they often reraise to try to isolate themselves against a single opponent? What kinds of hands do they show down at the river? Do they usually play only big pairs, or are they as likely to play middle pairs or suited connectors?

Once you have figured out how your opponents play, it's much easier to play against them. For example, if a tight player raises when she comes into the pot, you don't usually want to get involved with her. There are exceptions, of course. You might want to take a flop with a marginal hand against a tight opponent who only plays big pairs *if* she hasn't raised too much and has a lot of chips in front of her. In that case, if you have a hand such as 7-5 suited, you may be able to break her if you hit the flop. Now suppose a loose player brings it in for a raise and you don't have much of a hand. You know he's likely to raise with almost anything. You might reraise him whether you have a strong hand or not. In other words, make moves that you think will win the pot for you against the type of opponent you are facing.

Varying your play according to the situation—the next topic on my list—requires that you know something about the way your opponents usually play. And you can only do that if you have been carefully watching everything that has happened at the table.

VARY YOUR STYLE OF PLAY IN DIFFERENT SITUATIONS

In my travels with the WPT, I meet a lot of new No Limit Hold 'Em players. "Mike, I've read several poker books and they all talk about the importance of having good starting hands," a lot of them say. "But then I see these guys on the WPT and they seem to play anything and win with it. What gives?"

"There's a method to their madness," I usually answer. "They're playing more hands to vary their play in order to keep their opponents guessing about what they have." The top players understand that one of the most important traits of being a good No Limit Hold 'Em player is concealing the strength of your hand. To do this, you need to vary your play so that when you call or raise, your opponents don't know whether you have a hand. Simply put, you assume someone has big cards when she raises. Good players know this, so they will sometimes raise with small cards.

Experienced players don't play the same hand the same way every time because they know they will become too predictable to their opponents. For example, suppose I have A-Q against a guy who's dancing in every pot. I'm not going to be afraid to move all-in against him because I know he's a gambler. But if a *rock* (a conservative player) who only plays a hand once every hour comes into the pot, I'm not going to raise with my A-Q. In fact, I'm probably going to throw it away and not get involved in the pot. In both of these scenarios, I have the same hand, but I'll play it differently against a loose player than against a tight player. Different situations call for different strategies.

Raising with trash hands in the right situations is another way that top players occasionally vary their play. Players who raise before the flop with very weak *garfunkel* hands such as 7-2 or 10-3 are raising in an attempt to steal the blinds and antes. They aren't raising on the strength of their hole cards; they're raising to try to pick up the pot. They're hoping to get lucky and hit the flop in case someone calls their opening raise. For example, if the raiser has 6-3 and the flop comes 7-5-4, there's no way on earth that his opponent will be able to put him on a straight.

Of course, you aren't going to make the right decisions all the time about the strength of your opponents' cards. And you won't always be successful in varying your play in the right situations. Even the greatest poker players in the world make mistakes. Believe me, nobody is perfect on the green felt.

LEARN TO PUT YOUR OPPONENTS ON A HAND

Suppose you could play against an opponent in No Limit Hold 'Em with his cards face up on the table. He can't see your cards, but you can see his. Even the rankest amateur could beat the world champion if he could see the champ's down cards! Since that doesn't happen, you have to use other ways to determine what kinds of hands your opponents have. You do this by paying attention and gathering information.

Putting your opponents on a hand is one of the most important skills in No Limit Hold 'Em. The object is to figure out what their cards are to the best of your ability. Essentially, it's a guessing game, a game that you should be playing at all times when you're sitting at a poker table. Even when you aren't in the hand, you should be observing the players in the pot and guessing what they have.

Believe me, when you continue to guess at what your opponents have—when you watch the betting and gather information about what a player is doing, things like why she limped in before the flop and why she's checking or raising now—you will be able to better sort out what type of hands she has.

The process starts by watching your opponent bet before the flop and continuing to narrow her hand down from there. If she checks on the flop, try to determine whether she missed the flop, has a drawing hand or perhaps a second or bottom pair, or trying to trap by *slow-playing* a big hand. Play this game with yourself on literally every hand that is dealt during the entire session.

With enough practice at the guessing game, you'll eventually get it right more times than you might think. "He has a pair of jacks," or "I think he has a flush draw this time," you say to yourself. When the cards are turned faceup at the end of the hand, see how close you came to getting it right. Correctly putting your opponents on a hand is a skill that separates the top players from the rest. With practice at the guessing game, I promise that your game will improve dramatically and you will become a better poker player. And as you become a better player, you're going to win more often. All these things are like dominoes that eventually fall into place.

Certainly the dominoes all fell into place for Stu Ungar at the final table of the 1997 *World Series of Poker*. When the final hand came down, Stuey (all his friends called him Stuey) had around $2 million in chips and John Strzemp had about $800,000. Stuey had A-4 and made it $40,000 to go on the button. John called with

A-8. The flop came A-5-3. John led into Stuey with a $120,000 bet. Put yourself in Stuey's position: you raised before the flop and your opponent leads out on the flop when an ace hits—hmm. "What does he have?" Stuey wondered. He needed to put John on a hand to determine his best move.

Stuey figured that if John had an ace, it was a weak ace such as A-7 or A-8 (which is exactly what he had). What led him to think this? John didn't reraise before the flop, which he most likely would have done if he had an A-K or A-Q. Extend your thought process further: would John lead out and bet with *aces up* or trips? Stuey thought that if John had flopped either of those two hands, he probably would have checked on the flop to try to trap him, since John knew that Stuey was a very aggressive player. Not wanting to give John a draw just in case, for example, he had two fours or 5-4 suited, Stuey came over the top and raised John for all his chips. It turns out that John called all-in, a play that Stuey didn't think he would make. At the river Stuey caught a deuce, giving him a straight and his third world championship.

Many people thought that Stuey was lucky to win this pot. Yes, he was lucky to catch a card, but wasn't he unlucky to get called after he had moved all-in? What could John beat with his A-8? (Essentially, all that John could beat at that point was a bluff.) I love the way Stuey analyzed and played this interesting hand. Let me add, too, that even if Stuey had lost the pot, he wouldn't have been knocked out of the tournament. He would have had about $1.2 million to $1.6 million for John.

Ungar, who most veteran players (including me) consider the greatest No Limit Hold 'Em player of all time, was uncanny at sensing weakness in his opponents and putting them on a hand. When you can correctly guess what your opponents' hole cards are, you can win with any two cards. That's another great thing about No Limit Hold 'Em—you don't need cards to win!

BET THE RIGHT AMOUNT

Deciding how much to bet is an important decision that you have to make on virtually every hand you play in No Limit Hold 'Em. It is the *art* of the game. Here are a few pointers that will help you make correct betting decisions.

If you're the first one to enter the pot, you're better off to either raise the pot or throw your hand away. (I don't think you should come into a pot very often by just calling.) I recommend that you raise about the same amount every time. It doesn't matter what your hand is—whether it's two aces or the 7♥ 6♥ or a stone bluff—raise three-to-five times the size of the big blind. That is a big enough raise to force your opponents to have some type of hand if they want to play with you. Further, when you are consistent with your raises, they won't be able to tell whether you have a big pair or middle suited cards such as the 8♣ 7♣.

Many times you'll see a player raise with A-K before the flop. It's a good hand, one that you should raise with. But then the flop comes 10-8-6 and the raiser doesn't know what to do with the hand. He's lost at sea, a little bit afraid, so he just checks. His opponent automatically assumes that he doesn't have a big pair because he didn't bet the flop. So what does his opponent do? He bets to try to represent a pair because he knows the raiser probably has two big cards and didn't hit the flop. And even though he may have only Q-J, for example, he will take the pot away from the raiser if it's checked to him.

If you were the initial raiser before the flop with A-K and your opponent leads out on the flop—or if you check the flop and your opponent bets when it comes with something like 10-8-6—don't get stubborn. Simply fold and give up the battle. Wait for a better spot to go to war.

In No Limit Hold 'Em there is an extra element to betting, one that involves your feel for the game. At certain times, you don't want your opponents to call your bet, so you need to bet enough money to force them to fold. You want to do this when you're bluffing, for example. In a different type of situation, you may feel sure that you have the best hand, so you want your opponents to call when you bet. You want to get some value out of your hand. Now, you need to bet an amount of money that you believe they will call so that you can earn something on the hand.

Betting decisions are complex matters that you continually have to deal with in No Limit Hold 'Em. Practice and experience will help you considerably. You have to get some mileage under your belt before you can best determine how much to bet in all types of situations. However, when you are the first player to enter the pot, I recommend that you follow the general guideline and bet three-to-five times the size of the big blind.

FOLLOW YOUR INSTINCTS

In golf, you have to trust your swing. In poker, you need to trust your instincts and have enough heart to follow through with them. After losing a pot, how many times have you said to yourself, "I wish I'd followed my gut feeling and looked that guy up. I *knew* I had him beat" or "I knew I could have won that pot if I bet." Your instincts aren't just figments of your imagination. Instinct comes from knowledge and experience, things you remember from all the games you've played in the past. Great No Limit Hold 'Em players have great instincts that guide them in the play of key hands.

Part of instinct is getting a feel for the game. To win at poker, you must have enough heart to take risks based on your feel for the situation. Having a good sense of timing is also a part of instinct and feel. Your instincts kick into gear when you have the correct feel for a situation and your timing is right. That's when you can make moves on your opponents. Remember, you don't necessarily need the best hand to win. You can pick up a lot of pots just by following your gut feeling and showing some heart.

Let me give you an example of how an amateur player won a hand against a pro by following his instincts. At the Season 1 WPT L.A. Poker Classic, seasoned pro Gus Hansen was in the chip lead and raised to $18,000 with the 9♥ 8♣. Amateur player Daniel Rentzer called the raise from the big blind with the 3♥ 3♦. The flop came with the 10♣ 6♦ Q♦. Daniel boldly bet $18,000 into Gus, who called. When the 6♣ came on the turn, Daniel checked. Gus upped the stakes by betting $36,000. Daniel called.

At the river, the 2♦ showed up. Again Daniel checked to Gus. The Great Dane fired $50,000 into the pot on a stone bluff. To everybody's amazement, Daniel went with his instincts and called—with only a pair of threes! He felt confident that he had the best hand. He thought he had a dead read on Gus and had the heart to go with his instincts. Daniel moved into the chip lead on this hand, but Gus later regained it to win the tournament and $507,190. Daniel placed second for a payday of $278,595. One thing's for sure—Daniel showed tremendous instincts on that hand.

TAKE THE TIME TO THINK THINGS THROUGH

When it's your turn to act, you don't have to act immediately. You don't need to rush into making a decision about your hand, and you shouldn't. Take enough time to think things through.

I'm not saying that you should go into a lengthy deliberation every time it's your move. You don't want to slow down the game and annoy everybody by sitting there like a statue for three minutes. I'm simply suggesting that before you act in a *key hand*, pause to think over the situation—don't just automatically fold, call, or raise. Review the betting action that took place in front of you. Calculate your *odds* of winning if you call. Consider the kind of opponent(s) you're up against. Then make your move.

If you think before you act, you won't end up second-guessing yourself as often. You won't be saying, "Gee, maybe I should've folded when that rock raised from up front," or "If I'd thought about it more, I would've . . ." Those "woulda-coulda-shoulda" afterthoughts can take a toll on you.

"He's calculating the pot odds" is something you've probably heard me say on televised WPT tournaments when a player is taking his time before acting, and maybe you've wondered what that means. The next section is all about the odds and how they affect your betting decisions.

As a word of caution, there is also a saying in poker, "Think long and think wrong." Sometimes you can take too much time and outthink yourself. My advice: when in doubt as to what to do, go with your first instinct.

The basic principle of poker that you must understand before we begin talking about the odds is this: you want to bet your money when your hand is the favorite. Yes, your opponent might outdraw you with an inferior hand and win the pot, but since nobody can control luck, you should be satisfied that you did your best, no matter what the result. Know that if you put your money in with the best hand enough times, you're going to be a very successful player. Understand this concept first.

Then ask yourself, "How do I know that I have the best hand?" This is something that you need a little basic math to understand. When I say "basic" math, that's exactly what I mean. You don't have to be great at math to be a good poker player. You do need to have a basic understanding of math as it applies to poker to be a successful player.

First, you want to calculate the odds of getting the *outs*, the cards you need to make your best hand. For example, if you have a pair of kings and your opponent has a pair of 10s, and the four cards on the board through the turn are 7-6-4-2, you understand that your opponent has to catch a 10 with one card to go in order to win the pot. That's the only way she can win it. Since there are only two 10s left in the deck, you are about a 22-to-1 favorite to win the pot, which puts you at a huge advantage. (Because 8 of the 52 cards are showing, 44 cards remain in the deck. Two of those 44 help you, thus the 22-to-1 odds.)

Next, calculate your *pot odds* to determine the payoff risk. Calculating the pot odds simply means that you add up how much money is in the pot, then determine whether your hand is getting the proper odds to justify your calling a bet. If it is, you call. If it isn't, you fold. It's just that simple. That's how you apply basic math to poker.

Let's assume that you have an *open-end straight draw* with one card to go. You have J-10 and the board is showing 9-8-3-2. If you catch your straight at the river, you're going to win the pot. If you don't catch it, you will lose the pot. Assuming that there are eight cards (four queens and four sevens) that you can catch to complete your straight, you should calculate that you are about a 5-to-1 underdog to win the pot with one card to go. Being the shrewd observer that you are, you look at the pot to see how much money is in it. If your opponent bets $10, for example, there needs to be more than $50 in the pot for you to justify calling his bet. If there is more than $50 in the pot, you should make the call because you will be getting the proper odds. In other words, you're getting greater odds than you need to get.

Now, let's say that there is $100 in the pot. In this scenario, you're getting 10-to-1 odds on a draw that is theoretically about a 5-to-1 shot for you to catch to win the pot. Certainly, if you call a bet in this situation 24 hours a day, seven days a week, with every single card that comes off the deck, you will become a very rich person in a short period of time. When we say, "He's getting the right odds to call," this is what we're talking about.

What if you need to calculate the odds on the fourth card rather than on the river card? You have the same open-end straight draw and your opponent makes a bet at you. Maybe you're not getting 5-to-1 odds on your money; maybe you're only getting 3-to-1 or 4-to-1 odds on fourth street. "I'm not quite getting the real value I should be getting right now, but the pot's not over yet," you say to yourself. "We have one more round of betting to go. Assuming that I catch my card, I'm not only going to win what's in the pot now, I have the chance to win a lot more money, the money that's sitting in front of my opponent." This is what we call "implied odds."

Implied odds is one of the most important concepts to understand when you're playing No Limit Hold 'Em. It isn't necessarily the amount that's sitting in the pot right now that you're going to win; it's how much you might win because there's another round of betting to go. How much can you win if you call this bet and then hit your card? Can you win a lot more money? Calling the bet may even give you an opportunity to *bust a player.*

That's what good players are always trying to do. They are experts at calculating implied odds. They're trying to get lucky on a particular street before the river card by making a sort of gambling call because they know that if they hit their card, they have the chance to win a big pot. They will gamble on hands to try to catch a gut-shot straight, or try to catch some other type of draw, if they believe they can bust their opponent on the next round of betting if they hit it. And that's what you should be thinking about as well.

Sometimes it may look as though players at the final table of a WPT tournament are just gambling, when in reality they have calculated the pot odds and are making calls based on their calculations. They often consider other factors as well. For example, a player may call a bet on fourth street because he believes that even if he doesn't make his hand, he still can bet or bluff at the river and take the pot away from his opponent. Just because he hasn't made his hand doesn't necessarily mean that he can't win the pot. If he decides to apply pressure on his opponent by making a big bet at him, his opponent may not be able to call at the river. This is one of the beauties of No Limit Hold 'Em: you can win a pot without a hand.

To learn more about calculating odds, refer to the Poker Wiz at www.worldpokertour.com.

Play Aggressive Poker

When you're playing No Limit Hold 'Em, raise when you're the first one to enter a pot. Don't just call the amount of the big blind, which we call *limping in*. Take the lead—be the bettor or the raiser.

Here is an example that demonstrates the value of being aggressive when you're the first player to enter a pot. When you watch televised poker events, you sometimes see an expert player raise after an opponent has limped into the pot in front of him. Then whatever comes out on the flop, the player who limped in checks, the raiser bets, and the limper folds if he didn't hit the flop. But suppose the limper had raised when he came into the pot and the expert player had just called. No matter which cards came out on the flop, the first player could have bet and the expert would have folded if he didn't hit the flop. Remember that poker is all about betting.

Taking the lead will win a lot of pots for you. Most of the time, you aren't going to hit the flop with your two down cards. However, you might continue to bet in the hope that the flop didn't hit your opponent, either. Often you can steal the pot from him with a bet because most of the time the flop doesn't hit either one of you perfectly. This is the way experts pick up pot after pot. They play aggressively, they take the lead, they are the first ones to bet at the pot. And the first one to bet in No Limit Hold 'Em is generally the player who's going to be the most successful at the table. She's going to win a lot of pots when the flop doesn't hit her opponents simply because she bet first.

Generally, if you're planning to call if someone bets, you probably are far better off to make the first bet yourself. However, if you're planning to fold if your opponent bets, you're better off checking to him. In other words, if you're going to call anyway, you're better off betting in the first place because your bet might win the pot for you. Playing aggressively is key to your success at No Limit Hold 'Em.

Here's an example to further prove the point. Dave "Devilfish" Ulliott and Phil Ivey are not known for being timid at the poker table. It's a toss-up as to who is the more aggressive player, so it was interesting to watch when they faced off in the following hand during the Season 1 WPT Jack Binion World Poker Open. Dave had a huge chip lead over the rest of the field and used it like a machine gun to mow down the opposition. Holding only a J♠ 8♠ in early position, he opened with a raise to $16,000. Phil called the raise on the button with the K♣ Q♦, the blinds folded, and the dealer dealt the flop cards—10♦ 5♦ 3♥. With absolutely nothing, Dave fired in a $20,000 bet. Phil thought for a minute and then folded the best hand. In our commentary, Vince Van Patten and I agreed that Dave "earned the pot" with aggressive play.

MAINTAIN YOUR DISCIPLINE

Luck plays a role in our lives every day, and certainly luck plays a role in poker. We've all heard the saying "You make your own breaks." There's another old saying that goes around in the poker world: "If it wasn't for bad luck, I wouldn't have any luck at all!" We call it the "loser's lament." You'll also hear people say, "He got lucky to win that tournament," as though skill didn't play any role at all.

You might be wondering why I'm writing about luck when I'm supposed to be extolling the virtues of discipline. My reason for mentioning luck in the same breath as discipline is because the two seem to be joined at the hip in poker. The time when most players lose their discipline at the poker table is right after they get unlucky by either catching a string of unplayable cards or getting outdrawn. Of course, that's when maintaining your discipline and keeping cool can save the day and prevent you from going on tilt.

As important as it is to maintain your discipline under pressure, there are other ways that discipline can make you a better poker player. One of my favorites quotes came from Hall of Fame golfer Gary Player, who said, "The more I practice, the luckier I get." The key word here is "practice." And the key to practice is to take a disciplined approach to anything you want to get better at. It takes self-discipline to deal thousands of hands on the kitchen table and analyze how you would play each of them, and it takes real concentration and determination to read all the books and do computer simulations for hours in order to improve your game.

It also takes discipline to be able to wait for a good starting hand when you're running bad in a poker game. But if you don't maintain your discipline when you're being dealt junk hand after junk hand, cards like J-3 suited will start to look like pocket aces. You'll lose your patience, start playing too loose, and wind up losing your stack. The basic ingredient in patience is—you guessed it—discipline.

Discipline is your ace in the hole when it comes to playing consistently good poker. Don't leave home without it. Take it with you every time you play and you'll make more trips to the bank.

CHAPTER 5

How to Win No Limit
Texas Hold 'Em Poker Tournaments

If you're looking for something that gets your heart pumping and your adrenaline flowing, play in a No Limit Hold 'Em tournament. Poker tournaments are exciting, challenging, and potentially rewarding.

Wednesday night has become "poker night" across America when *World Poker Tour* tournaments air on the Travel Channel. WPT televised tournaments have elevated poker to a higher pinnacle than most of us ever imagined. People no longer view poker as a game that seedy characters play in the backroom of a smoky pool hall. Those days are gone forever. Nowadays the classiest casinos in the world sponsor WPT poker tournaments—places such as Bellagio, Borgata, Commerce Casino, and Foxwoods.

Thanks to the WPT, poker is now accepted as a recognized sports competition. In addition to poker pros, you'll find many prominent businessmen, women, and a number of college kids playing in every WPT event at all the top-notch casinos on the tour. And certainly Hollywood has embraced tournament poker. In fact, the entire nation has embraced No Limit Texas Hold 'Em tournaments. This increased interest in playing poker has not come about because of cash-game poker but because of tournament poker, the exciting do-or-die game that people enjoy watching on television.

As in other sports contests, the tournament playing field is even at the start of the game. Unlike cash games, every player begins with an equal number of chips in tournaments. You continue playing until you win everybody else's chips or until you lose all your chips. All you need to enter a tournament is enough money for the buy-in, which varies. The buy-in for most WPT tournaments is $10,000, but you can enter qualifying satellites that award a WPT buy-in for far less than that. (About half the players in the field in every WPT event have won their entries via a satellite.) Because of the luck factor, the great equalizer, even the rankest amateur has a chance to win the pot of gold at the end of the tournament rainbow.

On the WPT, virtually every event pays $1 million or more to the winner. That's huge money, but there's a lot more than that at stake. In addition to being seen on TV by your friends and family, there's the prestige and the bragging rights of being recognized as a poker champion who has bested the top poker players in the world, as well as the tremendous sense of achievement you feel when you do well in a tournament.

In the past, many of the greatest poker players in the world did not play tournament poker because the stakes they played for in the cash games were much higher than what tournament play had to offer. But today even the greatest cash-game players are playing the events on the WPT because the prize money is so large. It's exciting to see the top pros play, but you don't have to be one yourself to enter a WPT tournament. When you plunk your buy-in money on the tournament table, you have a theoretically equal opportunity to win, though you're going to have to play strong poker for multiple sessions to come out on top.

Age, sex, race, religion, education—none of those things are important to your success at poker because everybody is equal on the green felt. In fact, poker is one of the biggest "equal-opportunity employers" in the world. Poker players can climb up the ladder and make more money based on their own skills. They don't have to wait to be promoted by the boss—they can promote themselves when they think they're ready to move up to a higher-limit game.

We all like to be recognized for our achievements at something that is significant to us. To some players who already have success-ful careers outside of poker, the joy of tournament poker is the challenge of starting on equal footing against good players and seeing if they can beat them. Winning money isn't necessarily the object of the game to these folks—it is the conquest of victory in friendly competition that they're after. Tournament poker gives them a way to achieve a new goal and take pride in their accom-plishments.

If poker is your hobby, you enjoy having your peers and friends recognize you as a successful poker player, right? But even if you win a ton of money playing cash games, other than the few people sitting at your table, who knows about it? Who's there to pat you on the back and tell you what a great job you did? When you get good tournament results, you win the well-deserved recognition that comes with the territory. It's sweet when you can take home the cash, but placing that trophy on the mantelpiece is the icing on the cake. It is your symbol of success.

How Tournaments Work

Unlike other major sporting events, there are no qualification re-quirements to enter a tournament other than the amount of the buy-in; everyone is welcome. That's why you see such a wide vari-ety of players at the WPT final tables on television—newcomers battling veterans, youngsters competing with grandmothers, con-struction workers against dot-com moguls. Tournament poker plays no favorites.

Everyone receives the same number of chips to start with, so the playing field is even at the beginning—but not for long. The play progresses just as it does in cash games with one major exception: the blinds and *antes* (the limits) increase in graduated increments at predetermined times. As the blinds and antes continue to rise, some players will increase their chip stacks while others will lose chips. Eventually, those players who run out of chips are eliminated from action.

The tournament sponsor charges a certain amount to cover the expenses of running the tournament. For example, if a tournament buy-in is listed as "$1,000 + $60," your total buy-in will cost $1,060. The $1,000 goes into the prize pool and the house keeps $60. Most tournament sponsors also retain 3 percent of the prize pool for dealer gratuities, which tournament players refer to as "tokes."

Most large casino tournaments use a computer program that projects tournament information on a big screen. Looking at the monitor, you can easily see the amount of the blinds and required bring-in bets, how many minutes are left in the round, how many players are still in action, and the prize pool distribution. Online tournaments place this information on your computer screen so that you can easily see it.

There are two types of tournament formats: freeze-out tournaments and rebuy events. Freeze-out tournaments, in which you make only one buy-in payment and receive only one allotment of chips, are the most common. In freeze-outs, you cannot replenish your chip supply—you must leave the table when you run out of chips. All WPT events and most championship events are freeze-out tournaments.

In a rebuy tournament you can buy more chips if you go broke, but usually during the first levels only (the "rebuy period"). At the end of the rebuy period, you usually can replenish your chips one more time by buying an "add-on."

A major tournament such as those sponsored by the WPT usually is comprised of several preliminary tournaments with buy-ins that are lower than the buy-in for the championship event. Some venues have smaller buy-in tournaments sponsored by the casino that last for one day each, while others last for two days. Most tournaments culminate with a championship event. The total of all the events on the schedule is called "the tournament." The championship event in WPT tournaments lasts from three to five days (with the exception of the annual $25,000 buy-in World Poker Tour Championship, which lasts for seven days).

How to Jump-Start Your Tournament Career

Whether it cost you $10 to play in a small tournament or $10,000 to play in a WPT tournament, the joy of winning is the same. That's right. Whether you're playing at the final table of a WPT event trying to win a cool million, or you're playing a single-table tournament online trying to win $50 or $100, the feeling you get when you win it is the same. It's that "I've done it!" feeling. You're the champ! Believe me, it's one of the greatest feelings in the world.

I'll never forget the joy I felt the first time I won money in a poker tournament. It happened in 1981 at Amarillo Slim's Super Bowl of Poker in Lake Tahoe in the seven-card razz event. When I got to the final table, I was nervous and excited. Although I finished in third place rather than winning the event, I still had that feeling of accomplishment and pride for making the money.

The Super Bowl of Poker only paid the top-three places, even if there were 200 players in the tournament. That's the way Slim did it for years. He was the last guy to hold out on paying 9 places or 18 places or more. In Slim's tournaments, first place got 60 percent, second place got 30 percent, and third place got 10 percent. I didn't win much money, only a couple of thousand, but it was such a thrill. Today, virtually every tournament has expanded its payouts to about 10 percent of the field.

I felt the same way when I won my first gold bracelet and $106,000 at the 1989 World Series of Poker in the seven-card stud eight-or-better event, and at the 2000 Euro Finals of Poker at the Aviation Club in Paris, France, where I won $185,000 and became the first American to capture the title of European Poker Champion. No matter how different the payout, the feeling of accomplishment and elation is always the same. The money may come and go, but the satisfaction and the memory of victory is yours to keep forever.

Now let's look at some strategies that will help you get a head start on winning at tournament poker.

STEP ONE: PLAY SINGLE-TABLE TOURNAMENTS ONLINE

If you've never played a poker tournament, I recommend that you begin by playing a small buy-in, single-table tournament at an on-line card room. At PartyPoker.com, you can play online tournaments for as low as $5. You and nine other players begin with the same number of chips and continue playing until one player wins all the chips on the table. First-, second-, and third-place finishers receive a share of the prize pool (50 percent, 30 percent, and 20 percent for single-table tournaments).

If the buy-in for a casino or online tournament with 10 players at the table is $10 plus $1, the total prize pool would be $100. In this case, the winner would receive $50, the runner-up $30, and the third-place finisher $20. Since online tournaments offer a variety of buy-ins to choose from, select one you're comfortable with regardless of your level of skill or amount of experience.

STEP TWO: PLAY MULTITABLE ONLINE TOURNAMENTS

Once you have become familiar with how to play single-table tournaments, try playing in a multitable online tournament. A multitable event is simply a tournament in which multiple tables are in play simultaneously. You may be playing against 100, 200, or even 1,000 players. If 100 players sign up to play in a multitable tournament, 10 tournament tables with 10 players seated at each table will be playing at the same time.

You will get a lot of valuable experience playing multitable tournaments. And the more experience you have under your belt, the better tournament player you will become. As you progress, you will learn the importance of survival and how vital it is to gather chips. Eventually, you will feel the excitement of getting into the money for the first time.

It feels wonderful when you win a couple thousand bucks in a tournament that only cost you $20 to enter. That kind of win is possible online, because so many players sign up to play. But in truth, even if you don't win a penny, just the experience and the entertainment for the evening is worth the $20. It's great entertainment for about the same price as going to the movies. In poker tournaments, you do get a bang for your buck.

STEP THREE: PLAY A MULTITABLE TOURNAMENT IN A REGULAR CASINO

Once you have played a few multitable tournaments online, it's time to spread your wings and play in a tournament in a casino. Most daily and weekly casino tournaments are multitable events. Since you've already played multitable events online to get some experience under your belt, you will be comfortable with the structure and won't be intimidated by playing against so many opponents. Just remember this: regardless of the number of players in the tournament, only worry about and concentrate on the people at your table. Beat that table and you will continue to advance in the tournament.

The daily and weekly multitable tournaments in casinos are generally not expensive to play. You can buy into a multitable casino tournament for as little as $20 in most poker rooms (some venues also offer $20 rebuys).

One of the great things about tournament poker is that you know how much it's going to cost you to play in advance, whereas in a cash game you don't know what it's going to cost to play. It could cost you $20, $50, $200, or $300 to play a cash game. But if the tournament buy-in is $20, you know that's all your play is going to cost you. In other words, there is a fixed amount that you can lose, and you know that before you ever sit down and start to play. In traditional casinos as well as online casinos, you will find tournaments that easily fit any budget.

When you walk into a poker room, you should know what your

budget is in advance and have a pretty good idea about what game and limits you're going to play. The same thing applies to poker tournaments. For example, suppose you have committed $100 to playing tournaments, but the buy-in for the tournament you'd like to play is $300. In that case, you might choose to play a $30 satellite to try to win a seat in the tournament. Here's where your online experience in single-table tournaments will pay dividends for you.

SUPER SATELLITES

Super satellites are qualifying tournaments for a much larger event. Many multitable tournaments are super satellites. You can win a seat for a major tournament such as a WPT event by placing among the top finishers in a super satellite. The number of seats that a super satellite awards for the big tournament depends on the number of people who play in the satellite (along with rebuys where applicable). For example, if 200 players pay $500 each to enter a super satellite that awards seats into a $10,000 buy-in WPT tournament, the super satellite will award 10 seats for that event.

A casino also may offer single-table satellites in which you can win a seat in a much larger buy-in tournament. For example, 10 players may buy in for $20 each to win a $200 entry fee into a bigger tournament. In this case, only the winner would receive a seat in the main event. Casinos spread super satellites and one-table satellites to build the number of entries and increase the prize pool for their big tournaments, as well as to provide the "little guy" an opportunity to go for the gusto and grab the brass ring.

About half the players in the field in every WPT event get there by winning a satellite. And many players who have won their buy-ins for WPT tournaments in satellites have met with great success.

CHANGING TABLES

When a table becomes shorthanded in a multitable tournament, players from other tables with a full component of players will be assigned to move to the shorthanded table. You may have to change

World Poker Tour Satellite Winners

MICHAEL BENEDETTO, a businessman who had played poker for only one year, invested $70 in an online satellite and won a seat in the Caribbean Adventure. He finished in fourth place for a win of $132,600.

TED HARRINGTON, a building contractor, won a $109 satellite seat for the Ultimate Poker Classic. Playing on the beach in exotic Aruba, he finished fifth in the tournament and won $68,920.

RICHARD GRIJALVA, a 22-year-old college student, won a seat in the $25,000 buy-in World Poker Tour Championship via a satellite that cost only $86. Finishing fourth, he put $457,406 into his savings account to pay his college expenses.

CHRIS HINCH-CLIFFE, a construction worker, had the time of his life after winning a $25 satellite and a luxurious cruise package for the PartyPoker.com Million. Finishing third, he flew home with $441,463.

The charismatic Juha Helppi is a poker dealer in Finland, his native land. After winning the WPT Aruba Poker Classic in Season 1, he appeared in numerous television commercials for a popular online poker site. In the commercials, Helppi displayed his likable personality and wit, in sharp contrast to the expressionless demeanor he uses at the poker table to veil his strategy. He also placed fourth at the WPT Battle of

the Champions in Season 2. In his spare time, the young Finn participates in Finland's National Paintball League.

Matt Matros, a 26-year-old Yale graduate and professional writer, took home $706,903 for his $100 investment in an online satellite when he placed third in the 2004 World Poker Tour Championship event at Bellagio in Las Vegas.

Casinos and online sites such as PartyPoker.com, PokerStars.com, and UltimateBet.com regularly hold satellites for WPT tournaments. Visit www.worldpokertour.com for casino locations and satellite dates.

tables several times in a poker tournament, whether you are playing in a casino or online. My advice to you is this: don't pay attention to any other tables in the tournament. Always focus exclusively on the table where you are sitting.

Multitable tournaments work like this: Assume that 100 players enter a tournament. Ten tables with 10 players at each table will be in play. We'll number the tables 1 through 10. When 10 players lose all their chips, the players from Table 10 would move to fill in the seats of the players who have already been eliminated at the other tables. Then nine tables would be in play with 10 players each. As players are eliminated, tournament directors continue moving players to try to keep the tables balanced as best as they possibly can. This process continues until one table remains in action.

When the tournament director comes over to you and says, "We're going to move you to that table over there," just say, "Fine." When you first get there, look around to see who has the most chips and who has the least, and immediately start paying attention to how your opponents are playing. Focus on that table and forget about where you just came from.

Suppose you have just been moved to a new tournament table and you haven't had a chance to get to know the players. I've already mentioned (but can't overemphasize) that the first thing you should notice is who has the most chips and who has the *short stack* (the fewest chips). For the most part, you want to pick your fights with the shorter stacks because even if you lose a pot to them, you're still alive and kicking. Picking your spots, knowing who to fight and who not to fight, is a skill that is key to your success at tournament poker, a skill that you will develop with experience.

Eventually, of course, all except one table of players in the tournament will be broken. The remaining table is called the "final" table. And believe me, that's where you want to be because that's where the big money is.

THE FINAL TABLE

When a tournament has a large number of entrants, players who make it to the last two or three tables usually will win a percentage of the prize pool. These tables are called "money" tables. If you get that far in the tournament, you have "made it to the money," which means that you will receive a share of the prize pool. Most tournaments today pay about 10 percent of the field.

If you survive and continue to advance in the tournament, you will find yourself at the final table. That's your goal. Once you get there, you hope to get lucky and win the whole enchilada. The good news is that you will have plenty of experience playing a single-table tournament because that's how you began your tournament career. Now you're simply playing a single-table tournament until one person wins all the chips. This is how you should think about final-table play.

To win a tournament, you must possess shorthanded skills. You must recognize that as players decrease at a final table, so does hand strength. This means you need to be more aggressive as players are eliminated. For example, at a full table, A–8 wouldn't be considered a good hand, but with two or three players left, it would. When you reach a final table, you will be very appreciative of the time you have spent playing single-table tournaments. That experience will pay dividends for you.

WINNING STRATEGIES FOR NO LIMIT HOLD 'EM TOURNAMENTS

Here are a few tournament strategies that will help you get the chips and, hopefully, take home the title, the trophy, and the prize money.

Pay Attention: Learn How Your Opponents Play

Paying attention and getting to know your opponents is one of the most important skills in tournament poker. The more you learn about how your opponents play, the better able you will be to beat them. The first thing you should notice at your table is who the loose players are (the wreckless/loose cannon–style players) and who the tight players are.

It is especially important to learn how your opponents play when they are in the small blind or the big blind. Knowing whose blinds you can steal will help you pick up chips to build your stack.

You must be aware of the players you can rob and those you cannot rob. Who's going to pick up his sword and do battle with you? Who's going to lay down his sword and just let you walk quietly across the sand? Winning players know how to pick up pots when chips are out there to steal. They know whose blinds to attack, and they know when to back off against people who defend their blinds. This is a key difference between winning tournament players and losing players.

"Defenders of the blind" are players who just don't like to give up their blinds. If you raise the pot from late position when they are in the big blind, you know you're going to get played with most of the time. Even if you raise this type of player from the small blind, she most likely will call you to see the flop. What's worse is that blind defenders will sometimes come over the top of you with all their chips. When there is a defender in the blinds, a loose player who's going to gamble with you every time you raise it, you might have to be a little more careful about raising his or her blind.

Lucy Rokach is a top-notch tournament player from England who is known as a defender of the blinds. She always sends a message to her opponents early in a tournament that she will not be taken advantage of when she is in the blinds. "I'll let someone take one blind from me," she once told me, "but if they raise me a second time, I'm coming over the top of them regardless of what I have." Lucy believes that it's well worth the risk of going broke to make it clear to everyone that they should not mess with her blinds.

In contrast, there are tight players who virtually will never defend their hands when they are in the blinds. They are your targets. When you're sitting in late position and nobody has raised in front of you, you should raise almost every time when a tight player is sitting in the big blind. Nine times out of 10, he is going to throw his hand away when you raise the pot, and you're going to *pick up* (steal) *his blind*.

Conversely, when you are in the blinds, you need to know who the robber barons are who will try to steal your blind. The best defense for that is very simple: you just come over the top of them with a reraise. If a loose, aggressive player sitting in late position raises your blind, just reraise her, no matter what you have, if you suspect larceny. You will be amazed at how many pots you will pick up by doing this.

Coming over the top of the raiser a couple of times in a row serves two purposes: (1) most of the time, you're going to pick up the pot with a reraise because the raiser is going to fold when you reraise him; and (2) he's eventually going to stop raising your blind. If you come over the top of your opponent a few times in a row, I promise you that he's going to start backing off. "Hey, every time I stick my nose in there, this guy's gonna raise me," he will finally say to himself. "This guy's not afraid to play a pot. I can't run over him." Then he'll start backing off and give you proper respect.

You're going to win most of the pots that you reraise in that situation. As important, you're going to put fear not only in him, but in the other players at the table as well. "I'm nobody to mess with!" is a good image to have at the table.

Chips Are Power

In life, the strong survive and the weak perish. Big fish eat little fish. In tournament poker, the same law of the jungle applies. Big stacks prey upon little stacks. Chips are power! When you have them, you must take advantage of their strength.

In tournaments we see the rich getting richer all the time. Why? Because the big stacks gobble up blinds and antes and their stacks continue to grow. Most players don't want to mess with the big stacks, so what happens? The big-stack bullies continue to pick up pots because the shorter stacks are afraid to confront them.

Remember that blinds and antes continue to increase in tournament poker. They may increase every 20 minutes, every 30 minutes, or every hour depending on the structure of the tournament, but one thing's for sure—they are constantly going up. If you're not at least holding your own, winning one hand per round, your stack is going to shrink as the blinds and antes continue to increase.

Broomcorn's Uncle learned this lesson the hard way. He was a legendary poker player who would never play a pot unless he had pocket aces or kings. As a consequence, he just anted himself broke every night. Finally, he would get to the end of the tournament and have to play a pot, but by then he was short on chips and nobody was afraid of him. Because he was always short-stacked, he never won. Playing like Broomcorn's Uncle is a sure sign of failure in tournament poker.

To be successful at tournament poker, you have to learn how to operate with a lot of chips in front of you, and you have to learn how to operate on a short stack of chips. You need both skills to become a winner. Naturally, you'd rather have a lot of chips to play with. When you have a large stack of chips, you're King Kong, you're the boss, you're dictating the action. Your opponents are afraid of you because you can break them. That feeling of power and domination certainly applies in tournament poker when you are the chip leader at your table.

The first thing you should recognize at every tournament table you play—because you're paying attention, the number one thing that you can do when you're playing a tournament—is who has more chips than you have and who has fewer chips than you. It is vital for you to understand who can break you and who can't. Ideally, you would prefer not playing against big stacks that can break you. You would rather play pots with players who cannot break you so that even if you lose a pot, you're still alive in the tournament. If you go up against a big stack and lose the pot, it's bye-bye, birdie. You're on the rail scratching your head and saying, "You know, I shouldn't have messed with that guy, he had too many chips."

Use your chips as weapons of mass destruction when you have a big stack. If you are the chip leader, keep pounding away at the short stacks and stealing blinds and antes, growing your stack even higher. This is an important skill that you can learn with practice. Constantly put pressure on your opponents by raising the pot. When you continually attack the smaller stacks, you force them to have hands if they want to play with you. Believe me, they don't want to fool with you, because you're the one player at the table who can break them and send them home—and nobody wants to go home when they're playing in a poker tournament.

If you're on a short stack, never give up. Fight to the finish. *"A chip and a chair"* is a famous slogan in the tournament world. It became famous when Hall of Fame poker player Jack Strauss won the world championship in 1982 after being down to one chip. If you find yourself on a short stack, remember the battle cry—"A chip and a chair."

Try to Play Small Pots in the Beginning

The late Stu Ungar, three-time World Champion of Poker, said to me, "Sexton, in No Limit Hold 'Em I never want to play a big pot. I just want to play small pots." He knew that because he could steal blinds and antes and "chop out" some pots along the way, his chip stack would grow bigger and bigger. If you ever saw Stuey play a No Limit Hold 'Em tournament, you probably noticed that during the first couple of levels, nothing much would happen. But as soon as the $25 antes came into play, his style of play changed dramatically. The more chips in the middle to steal, the brighter his eyes lit up.

The blinds in most No Limit Hold 'Em tournament structures go from $25–$50 to $50–$100 and then $100–$200. At the next level the blinds will be $100–$200, but players will have to post a quarter ante ($25). As soon as everybody started putting those antes in the pot, Stuey was like a crocodile—bang, bang, bang, his jaws snapped shut. He was Pac-Man gobbling up chips. Almost always, an hour after players started anteing, Stuey would own literally every green chip ($25 chip) on the table. He would have to make change in every pot because he had stolen everybody's green chips. He may not have had the big chips at that stage, the ones you're trying to win, but he would have nearly all of the ante chips.

I was talking with Stuey one day when a good friend of ours, Al J. Ethier, came walking toward us. Stuey used to joke with Al and me about what tight players we were. When Al got within earshot of us, Stuey loudly said, "Sexton, I had the worst nightmare of my life last night. I'm not kidding you, I broke out in a cold sweat and couldn't sleep at all."

"What was your nightmare about?" I naively asked.

"I dreamed I was playing Al J. in a heads-up, No Limit Hold 'Em freeze-out with no blinds and no antes!"

Al J. and I cracked up. Although Stuey made this remark in jest, there is a strong message in his statement.

Many of today's great tournament players aggressively raise a lot of pots. However, if you reraise them a large bet, they will often fold because they don't want to play a big pot. Phil Hellmuth is the top player who comes to mind here. Phil is one of the best at making what we call "chop" bets, tiny little bets to gather information about who's got what. But if anybody reraises Phil when he makes a small bet, Phil will throw his hand away most of the time. Just as Stu Ungar wasn't, Phil isn't interested in playing a big pot. He doesn't want to play a coin-flip hand (see below) for all his money. Phil just wants to chop away and gradually build his stack, taking little steps that lead to the top of the mountain. He doesn't want to put the whole mountain at risk at one time. I love that chopping style of play.

Like Ungar used to do, Hellmuth is constantly picking up pots, as are players like WPT champions Gus Hansen and Daniel Negreanu. These great players frequently put in small bets to try to pick up pots. By doing that, they build their chip stacks for the later rounds of the tournament. To play this style of poker, you must have great poker instincts and a good feel for what cards your opponents have (putting them on a hand).

Avoid Playing Coin-Flip Hands
Early in the Tournament

Early in a tournament, most good players would prefer not playing a coin-flip hand for all their money. A coin-flip hand is one in which the odds of winning are fairly even between your hand and your opponent's hand. It's where one player has two overcards and another has an under pair. A classic example is A-K versus Q-Q. In this scenario, if you have the pair of queens, you are favored to win the pot—but not by much. The problem with *race* situations like this is that if you lose the pot, you're on the rail, you're out of action.

Losing a coin-flip pot has far more consequences than the possibility of *doubling up.* Doubling up early in a tournament doesn't mean all that much—you still have mountains and mountains to cross before you can win the tournament. Staying alive is much more to your advantage than moving all-in early. You need to recognize that you can never win a poker tournament until you get to the last table. You can never win it at the first table, no matter if you win every chip on the table. You have to get to the final table before you can win a tournament.

Many players believe that staying alive is the most vital strategy in tournament poker. After you've played in a few tournaments, you will certainly understand how important survival is. Survival is the key—it's everything. Once you are out of chips, you can't buy back into the tournament. You go home scratching your head, saying, "Gee, maybe I shouldn't have played that hand. Sure, I was a 52 percent to 48 percent favorite, but look what happened. Now I'm walking instead of playing."

Learn How to Survive

Knowing how long to wait before you actually move all of your chips into the pot is a part of survival strategy. One of my favorite lines about tournament poker is one that Tom McEvoy, 1983 World Champion of Poker, wrote: "Your mission is to put yourself in a position to get lucky." What he means is that you want to do whatever is necessary to survive to the final table. Then you hope to catch a few cards, get lucky, and win the tournament. At the end of a tournament, the blinds and antes are so high that no matter how many chips you have, you still have to get lucky and rake in a few pots to win the event. This quote has become legendary in tournament circles.

A new breed of players is taking another avenue to success in tournament poker—they are playing a lot of pots and accumulating chips. They understand that it's far easier to win a tournament when you're the chip leader at the final table.

When you see some of the WPT champions on television—guys like Gus Hansen, Daniel Negreanu, and Antonio Esfandiari—it looks like they're dancing every tune. To play that style requires a lot of poker savvy. These players believe it's more important to attempt to accumulate chips than to survive. They aren't worried about making it to the money; they're only concerned about winning. And there's a method to their madness—most of the money in tournaments goes to the top three finishers.

One of the winning strategies in poker is that if everyone at the table is playing tight, you should play loose to try to pick up the blinds and antes. On the other hand, if several loose maniacs are sitting at your table, your proper strategy is to sit back and play solid poker, waiting to pick them off with a good hand. Play the opposite of how your opponents are playing and you may find yourself playing alongside Gus and Daniel one day. But one thing's for sure: you can't win it if you're not in it!

Fight to the Finish with a Short Stack

When I was playing a lot of tournament poker, I was known as a very good short-stack player—sadly, because I seemingly always had a short stack! But I knew how to fight and hang on for a long time with just a few chips. You might think of yourself as the general of an army and your chips as the soldiers under your command. Unfortunately, when you're *on a short stack*, your army is undermanned, so you can't play as many hands or play as aggressively as you might like to play. You want to survive as long as you can with your small army of chips until the cards start coming to you, remembering that you can't win it if you're not in it.

When you have a short stack, you have to wait for a hand. You need to be more selective when you play a pot. You can't get too cutesy. You're just hoping to find some good cards, get your chips into the pot, and, hopefully, double up. You must learn to protect every chip you have and fight with your life for it. I've seen too many players just throw away the rest of their chips when they lose a pot they think they should have won. They become so frustrated, they quit trying to win. That is such a bad thing to do!

Remember "a chip and a chair," that famous tournament slogan. It's been around a long time because it's so true. On numerous occasions, players have come back from having only one chip to winning the tournament. You *can* come back from a short stack—you're not out of the tournament by any means—so you must fight to the finish.

At all times during a tournament, you must know when the limits are about to rise, especially when you're short on chips. When the limits go up, it's going to cost you a lot more per round to play, so you have to step it up a notch and play a little bit more. Do *not* ante yourself broke like Broomcorn's Uncle.

At some point, when you still have enough chips to make your opponent pause and wonder whether she wants to call you, you must make your move—whether you have a hand or not. You can't wait until you get so low on chips that it's automatic for your opponent to call even if she only has 7-4 offsuit. In other words, don't wait to play until your opponent is obligated to call you. Recognize that if you are extremely short-stacked, you can't hurt her if you win the pot and that she has a chance to take you out of action.

You can't become so afraid of getting eliminated that you allow your stack to get so low that you aren't in a competitive position. When your stack dwindles to four or five times the size of the big blind, you have to move your chips in—not later, maybe even sooner. I don't care what kind of hand you have, you must move all your chips in while you still have enough power to at least create a little bit of fear in your opponents. If you have at least four times the big blind, you still have enough chips to make them wonder, "Do I really want to play this Q-9 to try to bust the short stack and take the chance of doubling him up?"

Don't whittle your chip stack down to less than that. If you let your stack sink down to double the size of the big blind, your opponents are going to call you, no matter what they have, because they're getting the correct odds to do so. Move your chips in while you still have a chance to win the pot uncontested. It is vital that you understand this concept.

Don't Be Afraid to Play Your Hand

The great players are not afraid to play a pot. In contrast, average poker players often are afraid to play a pot in No Limit Hold 'Em.

Even when a mediocre player gets two aces, he often just wants to push all his chips into the pot and hope somebody calls him. Many average players are afraid to play after the flop, on fourth street, on fifth street. They may be scared because they don't know how much to bet or what to do, or they might be afraid of their opponents, or of losing their chips. The bottom line is that their fear of the possible outcome of a hand prevents them from playing correctly.

If you think you have the best hand, try to figure out the answers to these questions: "What is the best way for me to get the most money out of my opponent?" "How much should I bet to get maximum value for my hand?"

Poker is all about betting. Sometimes you want to bet enough to get your opponent to fold; at other times, you want him to call. Your goal is to get full value for your hand. To do that, you must play some hands through the flop to the river. Understand this: to win a tournament, you've got to win pots, not just blinds. At some point you have to get in there and mix it up and win big pots. You just can't pick up enough blinds to win a poker tournament.

Suppose you look down and find two aces. If you have chips and move all-in, the chances are good that everyone's going to fold. It would be nice if you moved all-in and someone called you, but that's probably not going to happen. Even when you pick up aces or kings, moving all-in is not always the correct strategy because people will most likely throw their hands away and you'll only win the blinds. You need to get value out of your good hands. Don't be afraid to play a pot when you pick up a good hand.

One of the purposes of this book is to help you lose your fears. That's why I'm giving you these tips. As you gain more experience, your fear level will go down. With practice and experience, you will also not be so afraid to play a pot that you just play all-in poker.

Be Careful Calling All-In Bets

There is no defense against the all-in bet, other than getting dealt a big hand. When you're playing against people who move all-in almost every time they play a pot, your choices are very limited.

World Poker Tour Championship trophy and prize money

The WPT Arena

Hosts of the WPT:
Mike Sexton, Shana Hiatt, and Vince Van Patten

Aviation Club de France Final Table, Season Three. From left to right: Tony G., Dave Colclaugh, Peter Roche, Jim Overman, Ben Roberts, Dealer, and Surinder Sunar

**WPT Battle of Champions, Season One. From left to right:
Champion Alan Goehring, Howard Lederer,
Gus Hansen, and Ron Rose**

**Money flying as Ron Rose (the eventual winner)
prepares to go head-to-head at WPT Battle of Champions, Season One**

WPT Ladies' Night I. From left to right: Shana Hiatt, Vince Van Patten, Annie Duke, Runner Up Evelyn Ng, Winner Clonie Gowen, Mike Sexton, Jennifer Harman, and Kathy Liebert

L.A. Poker Classic, Season Two.
Left to right: Commerce Casino Manager Tim Gustin, Vince Van Patten, Shana Hiatt, Winner Antonio Esfandiari, and Mike Sexton

**Season Two WPT World Championship Winner
Martin de Knijff**

**Left to right: Shana Hiatt, Audrey Kania, Vince Van Patten,
Player of the Year Erick Lindgren, Mike Sexton,
Steve Lipscomb, and Robyn Moder**

**Season Three Borgata Poker Open Winner
Daniel Negreanu with runner up David Williams**

WPT Walk of Fame Inaugural Inductees Doyle Brunson, James Garner, and Gus Hansen

Mike and Vince in Action

Steve Lipscomb with WPT production team Robyn Moder, Kristin Cranford, Cindy Fraser, and Bren Fitzpatrick

Mike with Lyle Berman

WPT truck pulling into Las Vegas

Once your opponent moves all-in, there is nothing you can do. All her chips are out there in the middle. You can't outplay her. Your only choices are to play or fold.

When my opponent goes all-in, the only way I can play is if I pick up a big hand. That's the *only* way. For example, I'm not going to put my money in with 9-8 suited if somebody has moved all-in in front of me, because even if I make my hand, I can't win any more money from him than the amount he has already put in the pot. In situations like this, I know that I'm an underdog in the pot, so I have to *lay down* (fold) my hand.

You are essentially defenseless against an all-in bet—until you pick up *that* hand. There's a saying in poker that the guy who continues to go all-in wins every time but once. When you pick up a winning hand against an all-in player, he is toast. Whenever you call an all-in bet, you should think that you have the best hand before the flop. That's the key. You want to put your money in when you believe you have the best hand before the flop—period. The only exception is when your opponent is so short-stacked that the pot odds dictate that you call with anything.

If a player tends to be aggressive, reckless, and moving all-in every single time, the strength of your hand certainly doesn't have to be as strong as it would be against a very tight player who never makes a play unless she has two aces or two kings. If a player moves all-in 10 or 20 times in a row, you know she doesn't have a strong hand all those times. When you pick up an A-J against a habitual all-in bettor, you're going to say, "You know, I think I've got her. I'm going to gamble with her here. She's raised all-in eighteen times in a row. I don't believe she can beat this hand." And you're going to gamble with your A-J. Make no mistake, it is a guessing game, but when you think you have the best hand, you just have to buckle up and go for it. You can't be meek and expect to win a tournament.

Tight Players Don't Win Tournaments

"What is the best strategy for tournament play?" is a question that a lot of new players ask me. They want to know if it's better to play tight and last longer in a tournament, or gamble it up and risk the possibility of being eliminated quickly. My answer is that you have to play the style you feel comfortable playing.

If you're a conservative player by nature, you won't feel comfortable ramming and jamming. If you're an aggressive player and/or you believe that you cannot play your game unless you have a lot of chips, you will have a difficult time playing tight. Conservative play is all right, just as long as you don't revert to playing too tightly. I'll tell you this: you don't see tight players winning very many tournaments.

My tournament observations are that aggressive, relentless, attacking players do the best, solid players are next best, and tight players fare the worst—by far. Being aggressive is the ticket to the winner's circle in tournament poker. As we've seen time and time again on *World Poker Tour*, the aggressive players are the ones taking home the title and the cash. The players who are winning tournaments are usually playing aggressively and using their poker skills far more than almost everyone else. When they make it to the final table, they usually get there with chips, and that gives them a much better chance of winning.

Understanding that tight players don't win tournaments is a key concept if you want to become successful playing tournament poker. Rocks may last longer than most players, but they don't win. The players you see winning tournaments are the ones who aren't afraid to get in there and mix it up. Winners are willing to take chances. They are not afraid to risk dying.

Here's the way Max Stern expressed this concept in *Championship Stud*: "Poker is similar to life. You have to understand that at some point, you will have to die. And at the moment that you understand that you are going to die, you will have a life." This analogy definitely applies to your final-table strategy in poker tournaments. You must be willing to die in order to have a better life (a better chance of winning). At the final table, some very tight players clam up because they are afraid that they're going to get busted out. These players are not playing to win; they are playing simply to survive for as long as they possibly can. It is these players who you want to take advantage of.

Here's another important concept: if you're fortunate enough

to make it to the final table, the smaller the number of your opponents, the more agressively you have to play with marginal hands. A
marginal hand is one that ordinarily would not have a winning
expectation against several opponents. For example, A-8 offsuit is
a pretty good hand in a three- or four-handed game, but if you're
playing in a nine-handed game, you generally don't want to play a
hand like that.

It is somewhat misleading to novice players when they see people playing marginal hands like A-6 at the final table and winning
big pots with them. The people are playing marginal hands because
the table is shorthanded—they most likely would not have played
them in a full-ring game. They realize that the shorter the table, the
more strength marginal hands gain. Therefore, as the number of
players gets smaller, the more the marginal hands increase in value.
To put it another way, the hand value you need to play a pot decreases as the number of players decreases.

When you're playing against only two or three opponents, you
can't sit back and wait for two aces like tight players are fond of
doing. That just isn't going to happen, so you have to make things
happen by playing some of the marginal hands.

Bluff When You Think the Situation Is Right

Mustering up enough courage to bluff is key to becoming a top
player in tournament poker. Many veteran players say, "Without
bluffing, there would be no poker." Bluffing is far more prevalent in
big-bet poker (no limit and pot-limit games) than in limit poker. A
great bluff is a thing of beauty—it is an art form. There is no better
feeling in poker than when you pull off a successful bluff.

If you believe your opponent is vulnerable, think about ways to
take the pot away from her even when you probably don't have the
best hand. Do not be afraid to gamble in a pot when you think you
might be able to steal the pot from your opponent. In golf, you are
taught to trust your swing. In poker, you need to trust your instincts. Be like a lion: when you sense weakness, go for the jugular.

Bluffing is how players "earn" their pots. It's what separates the
men from the boys, the women from the girls. Good players feel

much better about the pots they earn than those in which they had great cards that "played themselves." The chips may stack the same when you win a pot with a good hand, but it doesn't feel the same as when you earn the pot by bluffing. A successful bluff makes you feel good about your game and confident of your instincts.

How many times have you wanted to bluff at a pot but just couldn't pull the trigger? The difference between most new tournament players and expert players is that the expert knows when to pull the trigger—and she does it. Here's a quick tip about bluffing: bluff at good players, not bad ones. Why? Because experts will lay down a hand when they think they are beaten. Bad players, especially those who like to play sheriff, are more likely to call with inferior hands.

Sometimes you have to follow through with a bluff on the flop by firing a second bullet on the turn and possibly a third one at the river. As Stu Ungar told me years ago, "Sexton, lots of guys can fire one shell, but not very many will fire two." In other words, some players will bluff at a pot once, but if they get called, they won't bluff at it a second time.

WPT tournament champion Phil Ivey knows how to fire two shells, as evidenced by his play at the Jack Binion World Poker Open in Tunica, Mississippi. The tournament was down to three players at the final table. Ivey was playing a pot against another sensational player, David "Devilfish" Ulliott. With the antes at $2,000 and the blinds at $5,000–$10,000, Ivey raised the pot before the flop to $30,000 with the 10♠ 8♠. Ulliott called. The flop came A–K–3 rainbow (three different suits). Ivey bluffed at the pot by firing in a $30,000 bet. Again Ulliott called. The turn brought a deuce, but that didn't slow Ivey down. He fired the second shell and bet $60,000. The Devilfish folded. Plays like this demonstrate the power of the two-barreled bluff. It takes heart to bluff—but to be a champion, you've got to have heart.

To Ulliott's credit, he is a world-class player who is able to fold a hand when he thinks he is beaten. If he had been an inexperienced player, he may have called Ivey's bluff—all the more reason to bluff good players, not bad players. You simply cannot bluff a calling station because he is likely to call just to keep you honest.

Watching a player pull off a bluff at a WPT final table is exciting. You have the advantage of being able to see the players' hole cards and hear the commentary that Vince and I add to the play of the hand. Of course, neither the bluffer nor the player he is bluffing has that edge. Here's an example of a classic stone-cold bluff that happened in Season 1 during the L.A. Poker Classic at Commerce Casino. Andy Bloch brought it in for $18,000 with the A♣ 8♦. Amazingly, Gus Hansen called with the 4♦ 2♠. The flop came 8♠ 5♦ 9♦, giving Andy a middle pair and Gus zilch. Andy checked and so did Gus.

The turn card was the 10♣. Again Andy checked, but this time Gus bet $18,000—with absolutely nothing! Andy called the bluff bet. The J♣ came at the river. Now there were three cards higher than Andy's pair of eights, plus four cards to a straight, showing on the board. Andy checked. Taking advantage of the perfect situation, "Gatling Gun" Gus fired a second bullet at the pot in the form of a $36,000 bet. Since Andy had received no help for his pair and was looking at a very scary board, he folded.

The live audience at our tournaments cannot see the players' hole cards, but I'm certain that television viewers gasped in awe when they watched Gus pull off this gutsy bluff against such an excellent foe. As I said in my commentary during this tournament, "It pains Gus to throw a hand away!"

Stealing the Blinds Can Keep You in Action

When you're playing in a tournament, you want to try to steal the blinds and antes to build your stack. When you have a bigger stack than your opponent has, she cannot tolerate losing her chips as easily as you can because if she loses an all-in pot, she's out of action. Therefore, the chances are good that she will not call a raise with a marginal hand and try to suck out on you on the flop.

There is no more critical point in a tournament than when you start getting near the money. This is the time when stealing the blinds and antes becomes much easier. For the vast majority of tournament players, just making it to the money is their goal, their dream, their mission. As you approach the money spots, most players start tightening up to ensure themselves of a money finish. They're not going to play many hands, if any. They're just hoping that somebody else will get knocked out and vault them into the money. Any wise, perceptive player is going to pick up on that, and he's going to shift into attack mode and start stealing blinds and antes.

I've seen players win world championships this way. A prime example happened in 1992 when the top 36 finishers were paid at the World Series of Poker. With 37 of us left in the tournament, they were dealing hand for hand at all the tables. Everybody wanted somebody else to get knocked out so they could at least get back their $10,000 buy-in and make it to the money at the WSOP. And nobody was playing a pot at any of the tables. Literally, over two hours went by and nobody went broke. Not losing a player for two hours is practically unheard of when you only have to lose one player to get to the money.

I was sitting directly to the left of Hamid Dastmalchi. Hamid was down to about $30,000 in chips with 37 players left. He saw that nobody at our table was willing to play a hand, so he started raising every single pot. He literally raised every pot! Nobody, including me, wanted to play. We were throwing our cards away and looking over at another table hoping somebody would go broke.

What happened was incredible. Hamid went from $30,000 to $125,000 in chips simply by picking up blinds and antes. He made almost $100,000 going from 37 players to 36 because nobody wanted to play a pot! And he went on to win that tournament and become the World Champion of Poker. There's no question in my mind that if another player had gotten knocked out somewhere along the line, Hamid most likely would not have become the champion. But because nobody played a pot anywhere, he continued to increase his stack by taking advantage of the situation. Was that smart or what? He wasn't sitting there just trying to get into the money; he was trying to win the tournament. This story is the perfect introduction to my final tip.

Go for the win! That's what you'll see the great players do. They're not trying to move up one spot or make it to a higher payout—they have their minds set to try to get to the top. Why? Because that's where the money is! To make the big bucks, you have to finish first, second, or third in a tournament. Making it to the money in eighteenth place is nice, yes, but it's the highest goal that a lot of players hope to attain. They just want to go back to their hometowns and brag, "I made the money, I made the money at a WPT event!" And many will be thrilled with doing just that.

The top players are never thrilled with that. The best players want to win! And for sure, they want to make it to the top-three payoff spots. They're not playing cautiously when they get close to the money. They're attacking, picking up blinds and antes, and increasing their stacks so that when they arrive at the final table they will have a lot of chips and give themselves the best chance to win the whole enchilada.

Even early on, every tournament player should be aware of what the average stack size will be at the final table. Your quest should not only be to reach the championship table, but to reach it in better chip position than the average chip stack. Preferably, you want to get there as one of the chip leaders. Never forget that in tournament poker, chips are power. When I ran statistics on it, I discovered that the players who are the chip leaders going to the final table tend to come out in the top spots far more often than not.

To fully illustrate the importance of reaching the final table with chips, let's look at the results of the 2002 WSOP. There were 35 events that year, but one of them was a shoot-out (in which no one had a chip lead going to the final table) and another was a heads-up tournament, so I didn't count them. Here's what happened in the other 33 events: the chip leader going to the final table won the tournament 10 times, finished second 11 times, came in third 3 times, finished fourth 3 times, and took fifth place or lower 6 times. Further, the second-place chip leader going to the final table won the championship 9 times and finished second or third 12 times.

These statistics show that out of 99 places (the top three spots in the 33 events I evaluated), the players who started out in the top-two chip positions grabbed 45 out of a possible 66 spots (first and second place). That is nearly a 70 percent success rate in taking home the big money. The results speak for themselves: chips are power!

Generally speaking, if you go to the final table on a short stack, you'll probably finish ninth, eighth, or seventh unless you get very lucky and catch a lot of cards. Sure, once in a while you'll see the short stack get there, but usually you'll be one of the first players out if you start with a short stack. Most of the time, it is the chip leaders who will be fighting for the title at the end.

Accumulating chips is vital if you want to make it to the final table in good-enough chip position to make a run at the title. That's why I suggest that you don't sit back just because you're in the money. This is the time to attack, the time to get aggressive. When everybody else has pulled in the reins and they're all sitting back waiting, hoping that somebody else goes out, that's when you can take advantage of the situation.

For further proof that "gambling it up" can be good, look at the results of the inaugural $10,000 buy-in No Limit Hold 'Em championship at the Five Diamond World Poker Classic at Bellagio in 2002. Over five days of play, I got an up-close look at the players. The top four finishers—Gus Hansen, John Juanda, John Hennigan, and Kassem "Freddie" Deeb—played lots of hands, far more than their share.

These guys don't sit back and wait for aces and kings. They don't even wait for one ace or one king! They are relentless in their attack, chopping out pots and increasing their stacks. Then, all of a sudden, they flop a big duke (the winning hand) when they're holding a garfunkel and win a big pot. Of course, even though they raise with nothing a lot of times, they may actually pick up a real hand and win a big pot. Their reward for their aggressiveness is winning a boodle. Granted, this aggressive style works best in no limit poker; nevertheless, watching the top guns play on the WPT reinforces my opinion that being aggressive is how to get the gold.

So now you're thinking, "Let me get this straight. I can gamble it up, play every pot, and win tournaments like these guys?" I wish I could say that's true, but I can't. There is a method to their madness. First, you must be a great player to use this style successfully—and believe me, folks, these guys are great. Second, you must know where you're at in a hand, have a feel for the strength of your opponent's hand, and be able to fold when necessary. And third, one of the premier strengths of these aggressive-style top players is that their opponents can't put them on a hand. That alone is venomous.

"If you know all of this, why don't you fire it up when you play tournaments?" some of my readers have asked me. It's easier said than done, I usually answer. It's hard for a leopard to change its spots, and it's hard for most players, including me, to fire chips into the pot like a machine gun. They don't call me "M-60 Mike." I know that playing aggressive is a good way to win tournaments, but I also believe that you must be comfortable with your style of play to be successful at tournament poker.

The main point is that the most successful tournament players go for the gold. They get to the final table far more often than their more conservative opponents—and that's what counts. Just as important, if they get there, they get there with chips, giving them a better opportunity to get the gold. Winning is what gets you fame and fortune.

Poker Statistics

• In most poker tournaments, 80 to 95 percent of the players leave with nothing but memories of an exciting game.

• The *New York Times* estimates that 50–80 million people play poker regularly in the United States.

• Poker expert David Sklansky says the best way to negate a more skilled player's edge in Hold 'Em is to frequently go all-in before the flop.

• Most poker chips are compression-molded by 10,000 pounds per square inch of pressure and cooked at 300 degrees Fahrenheit.

• If you're holding 7-2 offsuit, the worst possible starting hand, you might be better off than you think against pocket aces. You're only a 7-to-1 underdog, so good luck!

• The odds of flopping a flush with two cards of the same suit in the pocket are 118 to 1.

• With six players at the table, the probability that no one will be dealt an ace before the flop is 33 percent. In heads-up play, it's 70 percent.

CHAPTER 6

World Poker Tour Key Hands

In every tournament you play, you will have to make a critical decision about how to play a key hand. A key hand is one that turns the tide of fortune. If you win it, you feel the thrill of victory—you're king of the hill. If you lose it, you taste the agony of defeat—you're one sick puppy.

Here are several great key hands that pitted player against player in a battle of skill and luck at the championship table of World Poker Tour tournaments. Analyzing these hands will help you get into the minds of the top great players, and lead you to a better understanding of the fine points of No Limit Hold 'Em tournament strategy.

You cannot afford to ante and blind yourself down to virtually nothing before you find a hand to play in a No Limit Hold 'Em tournament. Take a stand and go all-in while you still pose some threat to your opponents. Make your move when you have no less than four or five times the big blind. If you have fewer chips than that, an opponent is going to call you with any kind of hand because the pot odds dictate the call. To make things worse, you might get called by several opponents, which will make it even more difficult for you to win the pot and stay alive.

Here's how Chris Moneymaker, the 2003 World Champion of Poker, handled the situation when he was short-stacked during Bay 101's Shooting Stars tournament.

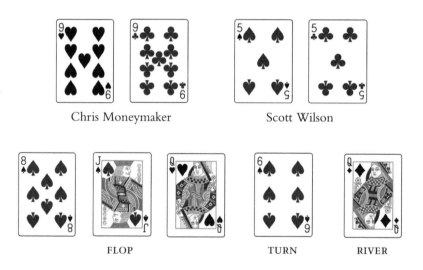

Chris Moneymaker   Scott Wilson

FLOP   TURN   RIVER

Chris Moneymaker was among the star players selected for the "honor" of having a bounty put on their heads in the Shooting Stars unique tournament. Every time a star got busted, the "bounty hunter" who broke him or her collected a $1,500 reward, plus a souvenir T-shirt and bragging rights. Chris was the last "shooting star" still in action when this hand came up.

Moneymaker found himself short-stacked with four players remaining at the final table. With only $209,000 in chips, he trailed

Chris Moneymaker   Scott Wilson

Phil Gordon, the chip leader, who had $1,517,000 in chips. Masoud Shojael, the second chip leader, had $422,000, and Scott Wilson was in third place with $271,000. The antes were $3,000, and the blinds were $12,000–$24,000.

Holding a pocket pair of nines, the best hand he had seen in quite a while, Chris moved all-in for the remaining $206,000 he had left after posting the ante. Suspecting that Chris might be making a desperation stab at the pot, or that he was trying to commit larceny, Scott called him with pocket fives. Adding some drama to the play, Scott picked up a flush draw when the 6♠ came on the turn. He needed a spade or a five at the river to win the pot, but got the Q♦ instead.

When his pocket nines held up, Chris won the $448,000 pot and moved into the second chip lead. As the result of this hand, Scott's stack was crippled and he later limped out in fourth place. Chris eventually finished second to Phil in a tough battle for the title.

READING YOUR OPPONENT

Getting to know your opponents is a key skill in No Limit Texas Hold 'Em. Some players are absolute masters at getting inside their opponents' heads. They can read them like a book, as we say in poker. These masters of poker psychology constantly observe every move the other players make. They remember how someone played a hand two hours ago, two weeks ago, and even two years ago in a certain situation. When a similar situation comes up in a hand they're playing against this same person, they know what he or she is probably going to do. That's how they're able to outplay most of their opponents.

Here's a good example of the importance of reading your opponents correctly.

Layne Flack

Howard Lederer

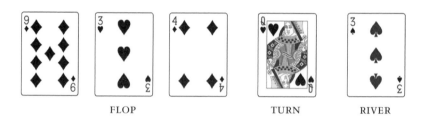

FLOP   TURN   RIVER

Members of the venerable Mashantucket Pequots danced around the table in ceremonial dress while prize money was stacked in front of Howard Lederer and Layne Flack, the two heads-up opponents at the final table of the World Poker Finals at Foxwoods Casino. Layne is known as an aggressive loose cannon to be reckoned with at the tournament table. (He may be viewed as a loose cannon, but he hits the target with his cannonballs. I think Layne is one of the most talented No Limit Hold 'Em players in the world.) Howard is recognized as one of the world's best high-stakes players. Howard had a commanding chip lead as they began their battle of wits and cards.

With the blinds at $3,000–$6,000, Howard raised to $18,000 from the button with the A♣ J♦. Layne called with the K♦ 7♥. On the flop of 9♦ 3♥ 4♦, Layne bet $25,000 in an apparent attempt to pick up the pot right then. No dice—Howard called with his two overcards.

The turn brought the Q♥. This time Layne checked and so did Howard. But when the threes washed up at the river, Layne probably decided it was time to take down the pot. He bet $35,000. Known as "the Professor of Poker," Howard thought for a few moments while Layne sat still as a statue. With no pair, Howard called! Knowing that Howard had read him like a book, Layne let loose with a faint smile as Howard raked in the pot with his *ace-high* hand.

COMING OVER THE TOP

In football, you often hear the expression "The best defense is a good offense." The same goes for poker. One of the strongest plays in No Limit Hold 'Em is reraising an opponent who has already raised the pot. This play is known as *coming over the top*. Coming over the top is the best defense against aggressive opponents. This move is especially effective in two situations: when the original raiser is in late position and you are in the blind, and when you know your opponent doesn't like playing big pots.

Raising and reraising in poker is an art and a science. Most important, raising is rewarding if you do it at the right time. Don't be afraid to raise and reraise in No Limit Hold 'Em—experience will help you learn when to do it and how much you should bet. Recognize that aggressive players fare much better than meek ones.

The perfect illustration of effectively coming over the top occurred at Bellagio's Five Diamond Poker Classic. Paul Phillips was sitting behind (to the left of) Gus Hansen, the most successful player in WPT history. Phillips specifically employed this tactic of large reraises against the ultra-aggressive "Great Dane" whenever Hansen raised the pot. Phillips's game plan worked to perfection as he battled from behind to capture his first WPT title. Now let's take a look at the following hand to see how coming over the top can win a pot for you even though you don't have the best hand at the moment.

Vinny Vinh   Antonio Esfandiari

They don't call Los Angeles "the Poker Capital of the World" for nothing. Southern California poker players are only a few free-way miles away from many of the finest card clubs in the world.

Commerce Casino, the largest casino poker room of them all, sits in the heart of the action. In all, 382 players made it to the L.A. Poker Classic, the WPT championship event at Commerce Casino.

During heads-up play for the title, Vinny Vinh and Antonio "the Magician" Esfandiari frequently raised and reraised each other. In this hand, Vinh raised the pot to $100,000 before the flop with an ace in the hole, a pretty good hand in heads-up action even with a weak kicker.

Vinny Vinh

But Esfandiari quickly came over the top of him with a reraise of $400,000. The raise was way too big for Vinh to consider calling, and he was forced to fold.

Certainly the Magician's suited Q-J was not the best hand, but he was able to pick up the pot by putting in such a big raise. The message is clear—aggression pays dividends on the green felt.

MOVING ALL-IN

Moving all-in is the power play in poker. When you push all your chips into the pot, your opponent is forced to stew about what to do. She is defenseless in terms of outplaying you. Your all-in bet requires her to pick up a good hand to be able to compete against you—unless you are so short-stacked that the pot odds dictate that your opponent call with any kind of hand. The all-in play will win you a lot of pots in No Limit Hold 'Em. But beware—this play works every time but once.

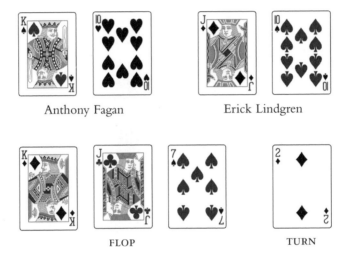

Anthony Fagan   Erick Lindgren

FLOP   TURN

The sound of ocean waves lapping the beach in exotic Aruba didn't have much effect on the six aggressive players fighting for the title and the top prize at UltimateBet.com's Ultimate Poker Classic. The final table was shaded by palm trees and "air-conditioned" by ocean breezes, but the action was hot.

Ireland's Anthony Fagan had been roughing up the field all day, but he made his only real mistake when he played—or should I say did not play—a pot against Erick Lindgren. He limped into the pot with the K♠ 10♥. Lindgren limped in right behind him with the J♦ 10♠. When the flop came K♦ J♣ 7♠, Fagan checked his top pair of kings. Lindgren bet $150,000 with the second-best pair, jacks. Fagan just called.

When the 2♦ came on the turn, Fagan again checked. After a long moment during which he apparently sensed Fagan's timidity and presumably thought he had the best hand, Lindgren went all-in. Incredibly, Fagan folded the likely winner, maybe because he thought Lindgren might have a king with a better kicker than his

10, or perhaps two pair. Whatever, it seemed to put him a little bit on tilt. Soon after that, he went on a string of all-in bluffs.

Fagan eventually ran into Lindgren again, who knocked him out of action in third place with A-K against his J-6. Fagan flew home from the island paradise $194,230 richer, while Lindgren went on to win the title and $500,000, enough to bask in the sun for a few more days. Moving all-in on Fagan was a key hand in vaulting Lindgren to the championship.

CHANGING GEARS

Changing gears means changing your style of play. You change gears to confuse your opponents. You want to keep them wondering what you have and guessing about how you're going to play a hand. Don't play the same way all the time—*play fast* for a while and then switch to playing tight, and vice versa. Players who always play the same style or at the same speed are fairly easy to put on a hand. And once you can put your opponent on a hand, you'll be making a lot of bank deposits.

Playing in the heart of California's Silicon Valley, Scott Wilson again tangled with Chris Moneymaker in the following key hand at Bay 101's Shooting Stars tournament, which attracted a field of

Chris Moneymaker

Scott Wilson

FLOP   TURN   RIVER

243 players. The table was four-handed with Scott on the short stack when Chris mixed up his play by changing gears from fast to slow.

World Champion of Poker Chris Moneymaker was on the button with pocket queens. Most players would raise with this hand from the button, but not Chris—not this time. He changed gears by slow-playing the two ladies. In other words, rather than putting in a raise, he just called in order to camouflage the strength of his hand. Masoud Shojael called from the small blind with the 6♥ 4♣. Scott Wilson, sitting in the big blind with the Q♥ J♥, knocked the table (checked).

The flop came J-5-9 rainbow. Masoud checked, and Scott bet $30,000 with his top pair. Chris came over the top by going all-in for the rest of his chips. Masoud got out of their way by folding. Scott called all-in, pushing all his chips to the center. There is no way that he could have put Chris on a hand as big as two queens in this situation because Chris had limped in on the button before the flop. He obviously thought that his pair of jacks with a queen kicker was the best hand.

By just calling on the button instead of putting in an aggressive raise, Chris won a monster pot. Scott was rewarded for his good poker skills when he exited in fourth place for a nice payday of $79,800. Chris picked up $200,000 for his second-place finish by adeptly changing gears at the right time.

WINNING WITH THE BEST KICKER

"It pays to have a kicker" is a common saying in poker. This is a lesson you will learn quickly when you first start playing No Limit Hold 'Em. In Hold 'Em poker, you play the best five-card hand between your two down cards and the five community cards. Sometimes, you and your opponent may have the same pair on the board. In that case, your kicker is used to break the tie. The kicker is your second card, and it comes into play when you both have the same pair.

This example from the Jack Binion World Poker Open near the banks of the mighty Mississippi River shows just how impor-

tant the best kicker can be when you and your opponent have otherwise equal hands.

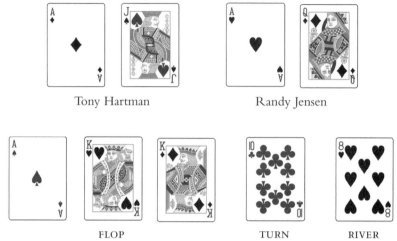

Tony Hartman   Randy Jensen

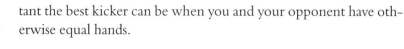

FLOP   TURN   RIVER

All six finalists were still playing at the championship table during this action-packed tournament at Tunica, one of the most popular stops on the tour. The cream had risen to the top from a
starting field of 367 recreational and professional poker players.

Tony Hartman   Randy Jensen

At the start of this hand, Tony Hartman was trailing the six-player field with only $123,000 in chips. Barry Greenstein was the chip leader with $990,000, and Randy Jensen was the second chip leader with $959,000. The antes were $2,000, and the blinds were $6,000–$12,000.

Everybody checked to Jensen, who was sitting on the button. He raised to $30,000 "in the blind" (without looking at his cards). Hartman went all-in from the small blind with A-J offsuit, and the big blind folded. Jensen then peeked at his hole cards, A-Q offsuit, and called Hartman's all-in wager.

When the board came A-K-K-10-8, they both made two pair, aces and kings, but it was Jensen's kicker, the Q♦, that won the pot for him. Jensen's A-A-K-K-Q defeated Hartman's A-A-K-K-J. Hartman collected $120,927 as he went out the door in sixth place. Jensen won $656,460 for finishing as the runner-up to Barry Greenstein, who pocketed $1,278,370.

BETTING AND RAISING THE RIGHT AMOUNT

Poker is all about betting. Sometimes you want an opponent to call, so you bet or raise her an amount you think she will call. Other times you bet, raise, or reraise a certain amount because you don't want her to call (when you are bluffing). Betting or raising the right amount is a skill that will take you some time to perfect. Making value bets is key to being a successful poker player. It helps if you know how your opponents play and whether they will suspect larceny if you make a large bet, or will suspect either weakness or strength when you make a small bet. In the following WPT tournament hand, Antonio Esfandiari and Vinny Vinh make an encore appearance in this section. Notice how Antonio used his skills in betting exactly the right amount to induce a call from Vinny, a formidable competitor.

The action was down to the last two players with Vinny and Antonio playing heads-up for the title. Vinh was in the chip lead. With the ante at $10,000 and the blinds at $50,000–$100,000, it was becoming very expensive to play a hand. Vinh limped into the pot (by calling the big blind) with pocket sevens. Antonio also just called with his A-3 suited, bringing the pot to $220,000. The Magician pulled a rabbit out of his hat when the flop came 3♦ 9♣ 3♣.

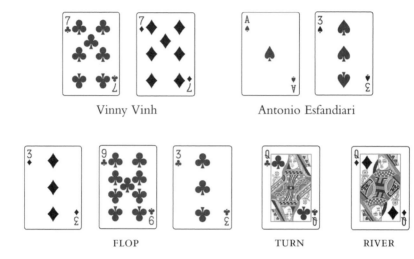

Vinny Vinh   Antonio Esfandiari

FLOP   TURN   RIVER

Antonio then made the perfect bet—a "massage" bet of the minimum $100,000. Suspecting thievery, Vinny raised him $200,000 with his two pair, sevens and threes. Antonio came back over the top of him for another $300,000. Vinny made the mistake of going for the reraise and set Antonio all-in. When the turn came with the Q♣, Vinny picked up a flush draw. He needed either a club or a seven to win the $2,640,000 pot. But the Q♦ came on the river to give Antonio a *full house*, threes full of queens.

Vinny didn't go out of the tournament on this key hand, but his stack was severely crippled. And Vinny's bankroll got a big boost when he took home $718,485 for his runner-up finish, but it was Antonio who went on to capture his first WPT title and $1,399,135! Betting the right amount at the right time was a key to his victory.

SEMI-BLUFFING TO PICK UP THE POT

A semi-bluff is a bet you make when you're trying to win the pot right there without getting called. When you semi-bluff, you always have outs (cards that you can win the pot with) in case your opponent decides to call instead of just letting you take the pot on the spot. In essence, it's a bluff tactic with hope in case someone calls you. Used properly, the semi-bluff can be a very effective play in No Limit Texas Hold 'Em, as you can see from the following example.

The WPT Championship is the highlight of the tour's season. The beautiful Bellagio on the fabulous Las Vegas Strip hosts the annual $25,000 buy-in grand finale. Known for its elegant and spacious poker room, as well as fine dining and exciting entertainment, Bellagio is home to the highest-stake poker games you'll find anywhere.

After plowing through a starting field of 343, the final 6 assembled at the championship table to fight to the finish for the top prize of $2,728,356!

It was quite exciting to watch this hand unfold. Many spectators (including me) thought it was the key pot that was played at the final table. It was a face-off between the chip leader from Sweden, Martin de Knijff, and young poker sensation Richard Grijalva, who qualified online for less than $100 to win his seat in this premier poker event.

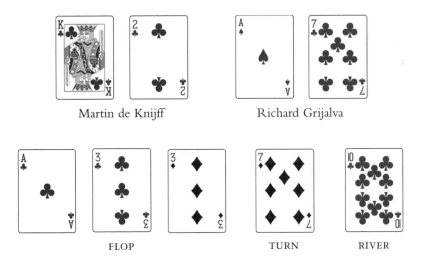

Martin de Knijff   Richard Grijalva

FLOP   TURN   RIVER

Four players were left in the biggest tournament in poker history at that time when Grijalva made it $275,000 to go with the A♠ 7♣. The others folded, and de Knijff called from the big blind with the K♣ 2♣. The flop came A♣ 3♣ 3♦, giving de Knijff the *nut-flush draw* and Grijalva the top pair. When Knijff checked, Grijalva bet $400,000. It was here that de Knijff decided to put the 22-year-old college student to the test. He moved all-in!

Grijalva was now faced with a very tough decision. Would you put your tournament on the line in this spot with a pair of aces and such a weak kicker? All you can beat is a bluff or a flush draw. At that time, de Knijff had a big chip lead and was making a power play with his chips. He semi-bluffed with the nut-flush draw in an attempt to pick up the pot right there.

Grijalva made a good read and called with all his chips. On the turn, he improved his hand to aces and sevens. With one card to come, all he had to do was dodge a club to win the $5,090,000 pot. But when de Knijff caught the 10♣ at the river, it was "Adios, amigo!" to Grijalva. He finished fourth and took home $457,408 for his efforts. Martin de Knijff went on to capture the title—and the $2,728,356 in prize money!

I actually liked the way both players played this hand. Remember, the beauty of the semi-bluff is that you have outs in case you are called. In this hand, those outs turned to gold for the Swede.

WINNING WITH A TOTAL BLUFF

Bluffing is one of the power tools of No Limit Hold 'Em. Players bluff more often in big-bet poker than in limit poker. In No Limit Hold 'Em, you can raise any amount you want to, up to the number of chips you have in front of you. When you bluff at the pot with a big raise, you make it very expensive for anyone to call you. In Limit Hold 'Em, you can only raise an amount that is twice the size of the big blind. It only costs an opponent another bet to call, so the bluff isn't as powerful as it is in No Limit Hold 'Em.

It is easier to bluff someone when the board contains "scare cards." Scare cards are board cards that make a better hand possible than the one you are holding. If you have Q-J in the hole, and the board cards are J-8-9-6-7, your pair of jacks doesn't look too good if your opponent makes a big bet, even if he's bluffing. And it's easier to bluff a good player than a bad one, because good players will fold if they think they're beaten, but weak players may call with almost anything.

The stone-cold bluff is an art form. You'll see what I mean when you look at this hand from the Season 1 WPT Championship tournament, in which two top-notch players were competing heads-up for a big pot.

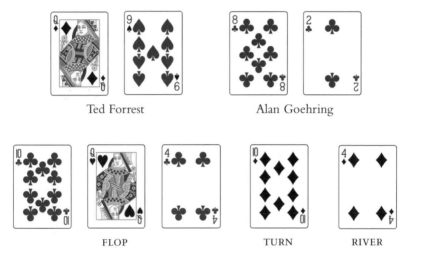

Ted Forrest   Alan Goehring

FLOP   TURN   RIVER

The Season 1 WPT Championship event at Bellagio was down to five players. With the blinds at $15,000–$30,000, Kirill Gerasimov folded under the gun. Ted Forrest limped in for the minimum $30,000 with the Q♦ 9♠, and Alan Goehring, the chip leader, also limped in from the button with the 8♣ 2♣. Poker legend Doyle Brunson put in the extra $15,000 to call from the small blind with A♠ 2♥ (unknown card), and Phil Ivey checked in the big blind with A♥ 3♦. Whereas final-table pots most often are played heads-up, here were four of the five remaining players in the same pot!

When the flop came with the 10♣ Q♥ 4♣, Doyle checked from the small blind, and Phil also checked from the big blind. Forrest bet $50,000 with his top pair, and Alan called with his flush draw. Doyle and Phil got out of their way. The 10♦ on the turn paired the board. Forrest checked his queens, and Goehring bet $100,000. Forrest called.

Now comes the "scary board" part. The 4♦ at the river made

Kirill Gerisamov

two pair showing on the board. Ted checked. Without hesitation, Alan bet $200,000 on a stone bluff, bringing the pot size to $635,000. Ted thought and thought. He even asked Alan, "Do you think I should call?" Alan responded with a touch of humor, saying, "I can't talk right now, I'm in a hand." After a few more moments of deliberation, Ted folded the best hand.

Thinking through the hand, Ted probably recounted that Alan had called his bet on the flop. Alan also had bet when Ted checked to him on the turn. What could he have? Ted realized that if Alan had called with a 4 or a 10, he was beaten. Obviously he didn't put Alan on a pure bluff—until after he saw the TV show.

And what made Alan think that he could pull off the bluff? He knew that Ted is a world-class player who is capable of laying down

Alan Goehring winning the World Poker Tour Season 1 championship

a hand when he thinks he's beaten. He might not have tried it if he had been up against a weaker opponent.

The great thing about No Limit Hold 'Em is that you don't have to have the best hand to win the pot.

WINNING THE POT WITH THE HIGH CARD

How can you win a pot by simply having the highest card? It happens! Sometimes nobody starts with a pocket pair and nobody makes a hand of any sort. In that case, the player with the highest card in his or her hand takes the pot. Usually it happens when players come into a pot with two high cards of different *ranks* or two suited cards. Then nothing comes on the board that pairs anyone's cards or makes a straight or flush for anybody.

This type of situation came up at the final table of the Party-Poker.com Million. Imagine yourself on board a luxurious cruise ship sailing the Sea of Cortez with 546 poker players who came aboard to play poker and party around the clock. But this time the game is Limit Hold 'Em, not No Limit Hold 'Em. In Limit Hold 'Em games, you can bet or raise the amount of the big blind, no more and no less. The final table was down to three players when this interesting hand came up between two seasoned veterans and a

Chris Hinchcliffe	Erick Lindgren	Daniel Negreanu

FLOP	TURN	RIVER

recreational player who had won his $7,000 buy-in via a Party Poker.com online satellite.

Due to the structured Limit Hold 'Em game, the action whipped along at a rapid pace. Chris Hinchcliffe, an audience favorite, had begun the final table as the dominating chip leader. He never changed gears and played very aggressively all the way, which proved to be his downfall (I liked the fact that he wasn't backing down from these tour pros, but it pays to put the gearshift in neutral at times). With three players left, he found himself trailing Erick Lindgren and Daniel Negreanu in third place.

With the blinds at $25,000–$50,000, Negreanu raised $50,000 on the button with the K♦ 6♠. Lindgren called from the $25,000 small blind with the Q♣ 9♠. Down to his last chips, Hinchcliffe pushed them in from the big blind with the Q♥ 8♣. It was a "family pot," as we say in poker when everybody at the table plays in the same pot.

Negreanu and Lindgren checked it through the river, neither of them making a bet at the pot. This is not unusual when the short stack is in the same pot with the two chip leaders. When they turned over their hands at the showdown, nobody had made a pair other than the open pair of deuces showing on the board!

Negreanu won the pot with his king-high hand, K-J-4-2-2. In other words, he had a pair of deuces with a king kicker, while Hinchcliffe and Lindgren each had Q-J-4-2-2 to make a pair of deuces with a queen kicker. A carpenter from Washington D.C., Hinchcliffe became the highest-paid amateur aboard the cruise ship, debarking with $441,463. Negreanu took $675,178 home to Las Vegas for his second-place finish. Lindgren had to find an extra suitcase to hold the $1 million he won.

SLOW-PLAYING THE BEST HAND

Slow-playing a hand means that you don't bet it for its full value. The slow-play is a deceptive move that you make in order to disguise the strength of your hand. It is one way that top players change gears in No Limit Hold 'Em to try to trap their opponents.

For example, sometimes a player will limp in from early position with pocket aces. He is hoping that somebody sitting behind him (a player who gets to act after you act) will put in a raise. That way, he can reraise (check-raise) with his aces, the best starting hand in Hold 'Em. If nobody raises, the player who has slow-played the aces still has the edge because his opponent(s) can't possibly know what a strong hand he has.

At the World Poker Challenge in Reno, the "Biggest Little City in the World," Paul "Eskimo" Clarke used the slow-play to trap his unsuspecting opponent. Take a look at how the play developed.

Harry Knopp   Paul "Eskimo" Clarke

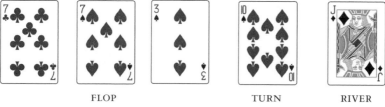

FLOP   TURN   RIVER

With the Sierra Nevada as the backdrop, Reno is just an hour's drive from Lake Tahoe, the most beautiful alpine lake in the United States. With one final chance to earn a guaranteed seat at the $25,000 buy-in WPT World Championship, 342 players ponied up the $5,000 entry fee to play in the World Poker Challenge. Only three players remained at the championship table when this hand came up.

Harry Knopp, retired from the U.S. Navy, had played good poker all day while entertaining the gallery with his chatter. Unfortunately for the retired navy man, he picked the wrong time to tangle with the chip leader, Eskimo Clarke.

Eskimo had been playing solid, fairly tight poker when he limped into the pot from the small blind with the 9♥ 7♥. Harry raised $50,000 in the big blind with the Q♣ 10♦. Loosening up his previously tight play, Clarke called the raise looking for "one of those flops."

He hit the jackpot when the flop came 7♣ 7♠ 3♠, giving him trips. Laying in the weeds, he checked to Harry, who bet an exploratory $175,000. Eskimo "smooth-called" (just calling when you have a strong hand), giving Harry a chance to catch up. The 10♠ on the turn was just what Clarke ordered, as it gave Harry a pair of 10s. Again Eskimo checked. Falling into Eskimo's trap, the retired navy man pushed his remaining $388,000 into the pot. Eskimo called. All Harry needed was one more 10 to win the pot. The J♦ at the river retired Harry for a second time, this time to the rail in third place, $155,202 richer. Eskimo warmed up with the $310,403 he pocketed for placing second to the eventual winner, Michael Kinney, who won $629,469 and a $25,000 seat in the Season 2 WPT Championship at Bellagio.

In poker, you'll discover that "all trappers don't wear fur hats," but some live in an igloo.

Playing a Drawing Hand

Many players like to mix up their game occasionally by playing middle suited connectors in No Limit Hold 'Em. You're better off playing big pairs, of course, but you can play hands like 9-8 suited or 8-7 suited when you only have to call a small bet before the flop. You're hoping to catch a flop and win a big pot.

Suited connectors usually are thought of as being drawing hands, meaning that you're hoping to catch a flop that completes a straight or a flush for you, or gives you a draw to a straight or a flush. Obviously, it would be nice if the flop came 6-5-4. You'd like that a whole lot better than seeing a flop with J-10-9 because somebody else could be holding a K-Q to make the best straight.

Here's a hand that illustrates the danger in making a low straight when a higher straight is possible.

For the PokerStars.com Caribbean Adventure, 221 poker play-

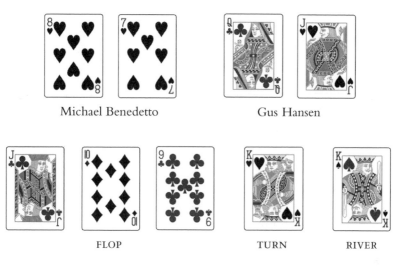

Michael Benedetto   Gus Hansen

FLOP   TURN   RIVER

ers boarded a luxury cruise ship headed for exotic ports in the Caribbean Sea. The WPT tournament was the main attraction, closely followed by snorkeling, jet skiing, miniature golf, and dancing till dusk in the disco. Four players remained at the championship table when this hand began. Only three lasted to play another round.

Satellite winner Michael Benedetto raised $20,000 with the 8♥ 7♥. Gus "the Great Dane" Hansen called the raise with the Q♣ J♥. Heads-up against the WPT's leading money winner, Michael probably felt his heart skip a beat when he hit the bull's-eye on the flop when it came up J-10-9, giving him a jack-high straight.

Gus, with a nice hand of the top pair and an open-end straight, was the first to act and came out slugging, in his usual aggressive style, with a $26,000 bet. Michael reraised all-in with his last $144,000 in chips. Gus called the raise. The turn card turned into a heartbreaker for Michael. The K♥ made the nut straight for Gus, leaving Michael with the "idiot end" (low end) of the straight.

Hansen, who went on to win the tournament, had pulled a hat trick, sending the three satellite qualifiers out in three consecutive hands. The first to go was Remco Schrijvers, a talented Dutch college student, who won $74,590. Next out was 21-year-old pro player John D'Agostino, who netted $99,450. Michael joined them on the rail in fourth place with $132,600 to soothe the blow of getting outdrawn.

WINNING THE RACE IN COIN-FLIP SITUATIONS

In No Limit Hold 'Em, coin-flip situations, meaning pretty-close-to-even propositions, come up frequently. Coin flips occur when one player goes all-in before the flop and an opponent calls. One player has two overcards and the other has an under pair (a pair lower in value than the opponent's two cards). For example, suppose Player A has K-Q in the hole and Player B has 8-8 in the pocket. In this situation, the pair is a slight favorite. In poker terminology, these situations are called races.

In order to do well in No Limit Hold 'Em tournaments, you need to get lucky and win your races, whether you have the two overcards or the under pair. Take a look at this hand played in "the City of Lights" and you'll see how important winning coin-flip hands can be.

Erick Lindgren   Jamie Posner

FLOP   TURN   RIVER

A lot of tourists visit Paris to soak in its romantic atmosphere, tour the Louvre, visit Notre-Dame Cathedral, and check out the Eiffel Tower. Poker players do these things and play poker at the elegant Aviation Club on the Champs-Elysees. In the most international of the WPT events, 91 poker players put their money on the table at the Grand Prix de Paris in Season 2. Two Americans, two

Frenchmen, one Brit, and a Greek tycoon made it to the championship table.

Erick Lindgren, a Las Vegas pro player, called the all-in bet of Jamie Posner, a British investment banker. Erick turned up wired nines and Jamie flipped over the A♣ K♥. Unfortunately for Erick, his favored pocket pair bowed to Jamie's two overcards when the flop came with the A♥, and he received no help for his pocket nines on the turn or the river. A little later in the tournament, Lindgren went out in fifth place with €53,600. Posner finished fourth and took €80,500 across the English Channel on his way home.

Jamie Posner

Chalk this race up to the Brit, but chalk the tournament win up to the French. David Benyamine, a former junior tennis champion who won his tournament seat via a satellite, outlasted the international field for a win of €357,200 when he edged out fellow countryman and terrific poker player, Jan Boubli. Although he finished fifth in Paris, Lindgren went on to capture two WPT titles in Season 2 and the WPT Player of the Year award.

FIGHTING TO THE FINISH WITH A SHORT STACK

Even when you're very short on chips in a tournament, fight to the finish. Never give up. Many times all you have to do is double up a couple of times to get right back into the ball game. Put up a good fight and, if you get lucky, you might be able to get right back in the thick of the action with some chips. The following hand demon-strates how a highly respected pro player who had been playing a patient and controlled game of No Limit Hold 'Em came out slug-ging in a daring duel to the finish.

Playing heads–up against Paul Phillips in the Five Diamond Poker Classic at Bellagio, top pro Dewey Tomko was extremely short on chips. Phillips had a commanding chip lead when Tomko opted to take the bull by the horns by using the move-all-in strat-egy to try to gather some chips. He went all-in a remarkable seven hands in a row against Phillips, winning them all without a show-down. On each of these seven hands, he picked up the blinds and antes to build his stack. Sometimes he had the best hand, sometimes he didn't. If you're not called, it doesn't matter.

Meanwhile, Phillips patiently waited for a hand that he could call Tomko with. He knew that Tomko was a strong opponent even when he was way short on chips, and he certainly didn't want to allow him to double up. Then came Tomko's eighth all-in move.

Paul Phillips   Dewey Tomko

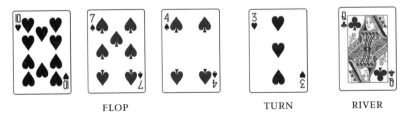

FLOP   TURN   RIVER

On try number eight, Dewey moved all-in with the K♠ 8♠. Paul called with pocket sevens. Paul hit the flop when he caught a seven to make trips. The flop also contained two spades, giving Dewey a flush draw. But when the 3♥ showed up on the turn and the Q♣ washed up at the river, Dewey discovered that you can slide only so far on barbed wire. Remember what I said about the all-in move working every time except the last time you try it? Paul took the title and $1,101,980, and Dewey had to settle for second place. Don't feel bad for Dewey, though, as he pocketed $552,853 for his efforts!

Dewey Tomko

HANDLING BAD BEATS

When you play poker, you will take bad beats from time to time—every poker player in the world has suffered from them. Trust me, the term "agony of defeat" sure applies to poker! We can't control luck, but we can control how we react to it. After taking a bad beat, it is very important to maintain your composure and avoid going on tilt. It's how you handle the adversity of bad beats that could very well determine your overall results in poker.

T. J. Cloutier is a tournament poker legend who knows how to handle bad beats in stride. Playing heads-up for the title against Chris Ferguson, he lost the championship event at the 2000 World Series of Poker when he took a bad beat on the last card. Chris had to catch a nine with one card to go to defeat T. J. Bingo! A nine slid off the deck at the river. T. J. showed tremendous class after taking that horrendous beat by simply stating, "That's poker."

It was bad-beat time again for T. J. at the Legends of Poker event at the Bicycle Casino in Southern California. "The Bike," as it is affectionately called by most poker players, is a legend itself and certainly a popular stop on the WPT. One of the original card clubs in the Los Angeles area, the Bike has a long history of some of the best poker action anywhere.

Three top players from a starting field of 309 were trying to add another notch to their belt. They already had shot down Chip Jett in fourth place, Farzad Bonyadi in fifth, and Phil Laak in sixth.

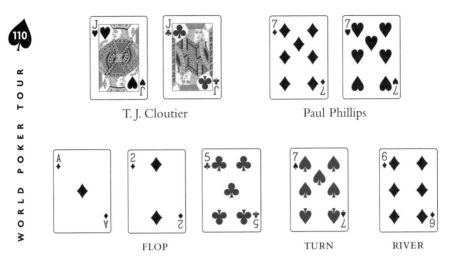

T. J. Cloutier   Paul Phillips

FLOP   TURN   RIVER

Only the Aussie Mel Judah, the dot-com whiz Paul Phillips, and the football player turned Texas road gambler T. J. Cloutier were left standing—make that sitting—at the championship table when T. J. played a monster pot with Paul. They both went all-in before the flop—T. J. with pocket jacks and Paul with a *wired pair* of sevens—and Mel got out of their way.

Things looked good for T. J.'s jacks when the A♦ 2♦ 5♣ came off the deck. But when Paul hit a *walking stick*—a seven— on the turn, T. J. walked to the rail in third place. He packed $146,775 in his bags and headed back to Dallas. Paul, who started the final table with a big chip lead, pocketed $293,550 for his runner-up finish to the wily Judah, who moved up from fifth position in the starting chip count to win the title and $579,375.

Poker can be cruel at times. It was another bad beat for T. J. at a critical time in a major championship. When you take a bad beat, try saying what T. J. said: "That's poker!"

T. J. Cloutier

People often ask me, "What is the most interesting hand you've seen on the World Poker Tour?" A lot of unique hands have been played on the WPT, but one of the most over-the-top hands occurred at the Jack Binion World Poker Open, because of the players involved in the pot and the crucial timing of the hand.

With four players remaining, it was crunch time. Each of the finalists—Barry Greenstein, Chip Reese, Randy Jensen, and James Tippen—could smell victory. They were savoring the prospect of winning a coveted WPT title and the $1.25 million first-place prize money, the largest in the history of the WPT at that time.

Reese was the short stack with about $280,000, with the other three players having over $1 million each. With the antes at $2,000 and the blinds at $10,000–$20,000, Jensen was sitting on the button, Tippen was in the small blind, Greenstein was in the big blind, and Reese was the first to act.

With the blinds about to go up, Reese decided to move all-in for $281,000. He later told me that he didn't want to raise it to $80,000 and then fold his hand if someone moved in on him. Jensen folded on the button. In the small blind, Tippen looked

James Tippen

Chip Reese

down at two queens and called Reese's all-in bet, leaving himself with $970,000 in chips.

Chip Reese

Barry Greenstein

James Tippen

FLOP

TURN

RIVER

Greenstein, the slight chip leader, found the A♦ K♦ in the big blind. He opted to go over the top and move all-in. By going all-in, he put Tippen to the test. Was he willing to play for all his chips? After considerable thought, Tippen decided to go for it and called Greenstein.

Greenstein flopped the top two pair and made the *nuts* (the best possible hand) at the river, *aces full* of kings. Obviously, this was the key hand of the tournament. And it was the first time in WPT history that two players were eliminated on the same hand with four players remaining in the tournament. Greenstein went on to win the event and $1.25 million, while Jensen finished second, earning $656,000; Tippen took home $328,230 in third-place money because he started the hand with more chips than Reese, who finished fourth, picking up $207,304.

Now let's get on to the real fun of posthand analysis by playing "What if?" What if Reese hadn't moved all-in? Chances are that Tippen and Greenstein would have clashed heads-up and Reese would have lived on with three players left.

What if Tippen had moved all-in immediately? Would Greenstein have called? When I asked Greenstein this question later, he told me that he would have folded if Tippen had moved all-in after Chip did. And notice that if that had happened, Reese would have won the pot with kings!

What if Tippin had folded when Greenstein reraised? Obviously, with nearly $1 million in chips, Tippen still would have been in good shape with three players left.

Now it's time to compare your thoughts about how the hand was played with my analysis of it. First, I tend to like Reese's all-in play in this situation. He forced his opponents to pick up a hand. Unfortunately for Chip, they did! Second, I thought Tippen made a great call with his pocket queens, rather than moving all-in. Third, I liked Greenstein's over-the-top all-in bet. Finally, I did not like Tippen's call of Greenstein's all-in reraise.

You may be saying, "Tippen made a great call, you idiot. He was the favorite!" As it turned out, Tippen was indeed the favorite, but I don't believe he analyzed the situation thoroughly enough. In my mind, for sure, there are only three hands that Greenstein could have had to come over the top: two aces, two kings, or A-K (possibly). I can't see him ever reraising with a worse hand in this situation. And there is no way he could have been making a move here, giving Reese (whom I'm sure he thought was his most dangerous opponent) the chance to triple up. Thus, in my mind, two queens in this spot would figure to be a big dog much of the time.

As I said, though, I loved Tippen's call of Reese's $281,000 bet—but only if he intended to fold them if Greenstein came over the top behind him. That's something Tippen didn't do. The bottom line is that if you call initially with queens and are also going to call an all-in reraise with them, you're better off to just go ahead and move all-in immediately. In this case, Greenstein said he would have folded his A-K.

Analyzing the strategies that you see world-class players use in WPT tournaments is a great way to learn from the pros. When you can get inside their heads and figure out why they played a hand a certain way, the lightbulbs come on—"Aha, now I get it!"

CHAPTER 7

World Poker Tour Final-Table Players

What does it take to make it to the final table of a World Poker Tour tournament? Skill mixed with just a little bit of luck—plus enough physical endurance to remain competitive during a three- to five-day battle for the fame and fortune that WPT final-table players enjoy. Meet some of the outstanding men and women who have played for the championship in WPT tournaments.

A former junior tennis star, Frenchman DAVID BENYAMINE turned his competitive instincts to poker in his teens after a back injury stalled his career on the courts. The native of southern France primarily plays high-stakes cash games and WPT tournaments. Benyamine credits his success at the tables to his intense desire to continually improve his game. "Poker is a lot about knowing yourself," he says. "I think I don't know myself well enough now."

Season 2: Grand Prix de Paris, 1st; Season 1: L.A. Poker Classic, 6th

A legend in the world of poker, septuagenarian DOYLE "TEXAS DOLLY" BRUNSON was one of the original road gamblers who made his living in rough-and-tumble Texas towns on the poker circuit of yesteryear. Brunson is a member of the Poker Hall of Fame and the winner of nine championship titles at the World Series of Poker. However, his biggest claim to fame may be *Super System*, the landmark book he coauthored and self-published in the 1970s, long considered to be the bible of poker instruction. The WPT added a tournament to its Season 3 tour in his honor, the Doyle Brunson North American Poker Championship at Bellagio in Las Vegas, where Brunson lives with Louise, his wife of 50 years,

Season 3: Legends of Poker, 1st; Season 1: WPT Championship, 4th

and their two energetic dogs. Doyle was inducted into the Poker Walk of Fame, located at Commerce Casino, in 2004. He also won the WPT Legends of Poker events at Bicycle Casino in August 2004.

ANNIE DUKE didn't always know she would become a professional poker player. As a student at Columbia University, where she had a double major in English and psychology, Duke intended to become a professor. It wasn't until she was in graduate school that her brother, poker pro Howard Lederer, taught

Season 1: Ladies Night, 3rd

her the game that would change her life. Duke left school after five years to pursue poker full-time. She placed third in the first WPT Ladies Night and won $2 million in the WSOP's Tournament of Champions. Duke is the mother of four children.

Season 2: World Poker Finals, 1st; Season 2: PokerStars Caribbean Adventure, 2nd

Native Alabaman HOYT CORKINS, who now lives in Las Vegas, won a championship bracelet at the 1992 World Series of Poker in pot-limit Omaha. These days he concentrates on playing what he calls "the glamour game"—No Limit Texas Hold 'Em—in WPT events, where his trademark is a 10-gallon Stetson and western attire. His aggressive style of play has earned Corkins the nickname "Mr. All-In."

Season 2: World Poker Tour Championship, 1st

A bridge Life Master at the age of 21, MARTIN DE KNIJFF is a professional poker player and sports handicapper who plays golf in his leisure time. "This is a dream come true," the 30-something native of Sweden exclaimed after outlasting 342 other poker players—many of them considered the world's best—and pocketing $2,728,356 in the WPT Championship event.

Season 2: L.A. Poker Classic, 1st;
Season 2: WPT Invitational, 6th;
Season 1: Gold Rush, 3rd; Season 2:
WPT Bad Boys, 5th

A native of Iran, ANTONIO ESFANDIARI moved to the San Francisco Bay area with his family at the age of 9. Ten years later he started performing as a professional magician at private parties. When he was 20, he learned to play poker and met Phil Laak, who became his roommate and taught him the finer points of the game. At age 25, the affable and handsome charmer won over $1 million at the WPT's popular L.A. Poker Classic. Esfandiari's nickname? "The Magician," of course.

Considered "the Grand Dame of Poker," MAUREEN FEDUNIAK is the grandmother of five. An avid gardener, Feduniak was born in England and resides in Las Vegas, where she maintains a lovely English tea garden. She and her businessman husband, Bob, who polished their skills at No Limit Hold 'Em with the help of poker superstar T. J. Cloutier, regularly play WPT events. Feduniak also enjoys playing poker online and considers herself an instinctual rather than analytical player.

Season 1: PartyPoker Million, 4th; Season 2: WPT Ladies Night, 4th

Season 2: San Jose's Bay 101 Shooting Star, 1st; Season 1: Aruba Poker Classic, 1st

PHIL GORDON is a former National Merit Scholar who went on to become a dot-com millionaire when he and his partners sold their software company. After traveling the world, the brainy Gordon began honing the poker skills his aunt Lib, who recently died of cancer, had taught him as a child. The poker-playing philanthropist has established a charitable organization in her memory, Put a Bad Beat on Cancer, and urges fellow players to donate 1 percent of their winnings to the cause. Gordon is the author of *Poker: The Real Deal*.

BARRY GREENSTEIN is a poker philanthropist who has donated millions of his tournament winnings to charitable causes. The Californian is a high-limit cash-game pro and tournament player who earned a degree in computer science from the University of Illinois

Season 2: Jack Binion World Poker Open, 1st; Season 2: PartyPoker Million, 5th

before joining Symantec as one of its original employees. Greenstein left the lucrative company lifestyle to play poker because, he said, "I could make more money and control my own fate. I compete in the WPT to attract attention for my favorite charities and encourage others to give." Children, Incorporated, a child sponsorship program affiliated with schools, orphanages, and welfare centers around the world, is his favorite charity. Greenstein's nickname is "the Robin Hood of Poker." In fact, Barry won $1.2 million at the Tunica WPT final table and donated it all to charity.

A native of Copenhagen, Denmark, GUS HANSEN is considered by many to be the best young player in poker. A born gamesman, not only is Hansen a star poker player, he is a world-class backgammon competitor and an expert at a dozen other games. His aggressive style of No Limit Hold 'Em and willingness to take big risks with seemingly marginal hands can intimidate even the most experienced professionals. With three WPT championships under his belt in the first two seasons, the irrepressible Hansen's nickname—"the Great Dane"— seems especially appropriate.

Season 2: PokerStars Caribbean Adventure, 1st; Season 2: WPT Battle of Champions, 6th; Season 2: Five Diamond World Poker Classic, 3rd; Season 1: L.A. Poker Classic, 1st; Season 1: Five Diamond World Poker Classic, 1st

Season 1: Aruba Poker Classic, 2nd; Season 2: Borgata Poker Open, 7th; Season 2: WPT Ladies Night, 5th

JENNIFER HARMAN, a diminutive poker ace from Las Vegas, regularly plays the biggest poker game in the world at Bellagio and has won two gold bracelets at the World Series of Poker. Widely considered to be one of the best poker players on the planet, especially dominant as a cash player, she attributes her success to an "uncanny ability to get inside someone's head." Harman and her husband, Italian superstar hairdresser Marco Traniello, regularly fly around the world for their respective careers.

When he was 24 years old, PHIL HELLMUTH, JR. became the youngest player ever to win the World Championship of Poker and

has since added eight more WSOP bracelets to his collection. Dubbed "the Poker Brat" for his sometimes tempestuous behavior at the poker table, Hellmuth is the author of *Play Poker Like the Pros* and a video and DVD series titled *Phil Hellmuth's Million Dollar Poker System*. Hellmuth also writes a popular poker-analysis columnist for *Card Player* magazine. He lives in California with his wife, who is a physician, and their two sons.

Season 2: World Poker Finals, 3rd; Season 1: Gold Rush, 4th; Season 1: Aruba Poker Classic, 4th

Twenty-something PHIL IVEY is one of the most recognizable faces on the WPT with three final-table appearances to his credit. Known as a world-class seven-card stud player as well as a formidable No Limit Hold 'Em aficionado, Ivey has won four World Championship titles and finished 10th in the WSOP No Limit Hold 'Em championship in 2003. Before his recent move to Los Angeles, Ivey lived in Atlantic City. The avid Lakers fan likes to play pickup basketball in his leisure time.

Season 1: Jack Binion World Poker Open, 2nd; Season 1: WPT Championship, 3rd; Season 1: World Poker Finals, 4th; Season 3: Borgota Poker Open, 6th

Season 2: WPT Invitational, 1st; Season 2: Legends of Poker, 6th; Season 2: Bad Boys of Poker, 4th

PHIL LAAK is an emerging star of No Limit Texas Hold 'Em on the WPT. Laak's unusual attire at the final table—a hooded sweatshirt, which he periodically pulls over his face, and wraparound sunglasses—have earned him the nickname "Unabomber." In contrast to his physically active, eccentric behavior during poker tournaments, Laak is an analytical player who claims to be driven by "playing well, not by winning." His pastimes include judo, skydiving, and scuba.

HOWARD LEDERER, nick-named "the Professor of Poker," is a thoughtful poker champion known for care-fully calculating his odds of winning at the final table. Lederer and his sister, Annie Duke, whom he coached on how to win at poker, are considered two of the game's best high-stakes players. Led-erer switched from playing world-class chess to playing world-class poker when he moved from New Hamp-shire to attend Columbia University in New York City, where he stumbled upon the backroom poker games so vividly depicted in the movie *Rounders*. Ten years later he moved to Las Vegas, where he won a gold bracelet at the WSOP in 2001.

Season 1: PartyPoker Million, 1st; Season 1: World Poker Finals, 1st; Season 2: WPT Battle of Champions, 3rd

Lederer is a TV poker show commentator and the author of *Howard Lederer's Secrets of No-Limit Hold 'Em*, a DVD-video series.

ERICK LINDGREN won the WPT Season 2 Player of the Year title. En route to that honor, the 20-something champion amassed $1.5 mil-lion and earned a reputation as a formidable tournament poker player. He was an all-league football quarterback and MVP basketball player in high school, proving that competitive instincts come

Season 2: PartyPoker Million, 1st; Season 2: Ultimate Poker Classic, 1st; Season 2: Grand Prix de Paris, 5th naturally to the young Californian with the "all-American guy" looks. An avid online poker player, Lindgren won his seat in the PartyPoker Million via a $162 satellite tournament. He credits his success at poker to his "extreme patience, understanding what people are thinking and what they are likely to do, and some pretty good math skills." In his spare time, the photogenic poker phenom likes to play golf and basketball.

Canadian ace DANIEL NEGREANU won his first World Series bracelet at age 23 and hasn't slowed down since, adding five more WSOP victories and a score of other major championships to his résumé, including being named Best All-Around Player at Foxwood's World Poker Finals and Commerce Casino's L.A. Poker Classic. After beginning his career in gambling by betting sports and hustling pool, Negreanu moved his bets to the poker table in home games at age 18. When he turned 21, he crossed the border into Las Vegas to become a professional player. Often seen at the final table wearing a hockey jersey, the energetic and witty Negreanu enjoys playing fantasy hockey and golf. Negreanu pens a popular column for *Card Player* magazine with savvy advice and observations that have earned him a multitude of fans.

Season 2: PartyPoker Million, 2nd; Season 2: PokerStars Caribbean Adventure, 3rd; Season 2: Grand Prix de Paris, 7th; Season 3: Borgota Poker Open, 1st

Season 1: Aruba Poker Classic, 3rd; Season 1: Five Diamond World Poker Classic, 6th; Season 2: Party-Poker Million, 6th

With a last name that rhymes with "win," SCOTTY NGUYEN has been a winner ever since he hit safe shores after escaping by boat from Vietnam. The Las Vegas poker whiz won the World Championship of Poker in 1998 and has many other major titles to his credit. Known for his sartorial style, which always includes glittering gold jewelry, and his signature sentence-ending "baby," the ebullient Nguyen is one of the most colorful, as well as accomplished, players on the WPT circuit.

Dot-com millionaire PAUL PHILLIPS placed second only to Erick Lindgren in the WPT Player of the Year competition. The former chief technical officer of Go2Net.com, Phillips built the company and cashed out before cashing in on the WPT. Known for his suit-and-tie attire at the final table, the self-proclaimed perpetual student of poker says, "You're never done getting better at this game." After being a successful entrepreneur, Phillips finds tournament poker challenging and satisfying. His nickname? "Dot-com," what else!

Season 2: Bellagio Five Diamond Poker Classic, 1st; Season 2: Legends of Poker, 2nd

World Poker Tour Players to Watch

These players have come on strong in Season 3 of the WPT, and I think we will see much more of them in the future.

A poker pro from Marietta, Georgia, the 29-year-old JOSH ARIEH had a big year in 2004. After placing third at the World Series of Poker and winning $2.5 million, Arieh found himself at another final table—this time at the Borgata Poker Open at Borgata in Atlantic City. He again placed third and earned a cool $286,900.

ISABELLE "No Mercy" MERCIER has had many careers in her life. She's been a lawyer, a blackjack dealer, and a poker dealer. However, the job she's most known for by players on the WPT tournament player circuit is tournament director of the Aviation Club de France, a charter member of the WPT. Mercier quit her job at the Aviation Club in January 2004 to become a full-time professional poker player. Just in time, too— she won WPT Ladies Night II and earned a $25,000 seat at the 2005 WPT Championship at the Bellagio.

Pro poker player, amateur surfer, economics major—LEE WATKINSON has done it all. Watkinson became a millionaire in Season 3 of the WPT when he finished second in back-to-back WPT events. At the Mirage Poker Showdown at Mirage in Las Vegas, Watkinson took home $513,038. A mere four weeks later, Watkinson again placed second, this time to legendary player Doyle Brunson at the Legends of Poker at the Bicycle Casino in Bell Gardens, California, and took home $578,475.

DAVID WILLIAMS, 24, is an economics major from Arlington, Texas, who is not only adept at managing his chip count, but also the $573,800 he earned as a second-place finisher at the 2004 Borgata Poker Open. He also had a second place finish in the 2004 World Series of Poker Championship Event. Williams has been playing poker for seven years and calls it his "dream job."

Poker Quiz

1. What are the odds of getting a better hand after your opening hand?

2. If before the flop, you got A-A, and you're up against someone with K-K, how often should you win?
   - A. 62 percent of the time
   - B. 72 percent of the time
   - C. 82 percent of the time
   - D. 92 percent of the time

3. You are dealt an A♥ 4♦, and your opponent has an A♣ 2♠. Who is the favorite to win all the chips?

4. You hold an A♥ K♥; what are the odds you'll flop a royal flush?

5. Which of these movies does not involve poker?
   - A. *The Big Blind*
   - B. *Wanda Nevada*
   - C. *Queen High*
   - D. *Raising the Stakes*

6. Which is not a type of poker?
   - A. Razz
   - B. Manila
   - C. Bangkok
   - D. Omaha

7. What is "paint" when referring to a deck of cards in poker?
   A. Back of the cards
   B. Marked cards
   C. Royalty cards
   D. A new deck

8. How did Doyle Brunson get his nickname "Texas Dolly"?

9. What are the odds of a four of a kind showing up on the board?

Answers: 1. 50 percent. The moral—don't bet unless you have something to start with. 2. C. 3. Nearly 50 percent of the time it's a split pot. 4. 19,599 to 1. 5. D. 6. C. 7. C. 8. Jimmy "the Greek" Snyder misread "Doyle" as "Dolly" and the name stuck. 9. 1 in 54,145.

CHAPTER **8**

How to Beat Online Poker

Many old-time poker players don't consider online poker to be "real" poker. They think of it as a video game. To them, "poker" means sitting at a green-felt table looking your opponent in the eye.

In reality, online poker is simply a newer, different form of poker—and there's no question that it is the real deal. Like many other games, poker has graduated with the times into the computer era. At online poker sites, players from all over the world compete with one another in live, real-time games. The only reason online poker works is because it takes place in "real time." You are actually playing against real people "in the moment." You may not be able to see your opponents, but the action is real.

The beauty of online poker is multifaceted. Newcomers can

learn the basics of poker in free games before advancing to low-stakes tournaments or games. Online card rooms are open around the clock so you can get a lot of experience in a short time. And they provide you the opportunity to gain valuable tournament experience. The World Poker Tour and online card rooms expanded the poker industry by bringing thousands of new players into the game on a daily basis.

You Can Learn How to Play Poker at Online Card Rooms

Everyone coming out of high school these days is computer literate. Most kids have been playing video games since they were six years old, whereas in my youth there were no computers and no video games. When we played poker years ago, there were no poker books and no online poker rooms. I learned by playing in a live poker game, coming home broke, and scratching my head while asking, "What did I do wrong tonight?" Like everyone else, I had to figure it out for myself.

Today, the WPT and online poker offer a great way to learn how to play poker before you venture into a casino. You can learn how the betting works, the procedures of the game, and how to play new games you haven't played before, such as No Limit Hold 'Em or Omaha high-low split or razz. Playing online gives you a feel for the game.

Think of online poker sites as training grounds where you can learn how to play poker without any monetary exposure. That's right, folks, you can play poker for free online; you don't have to put up money to play. In a casino, you won't hear the floor man say, "Hey, come on in here and have a seat. We'll hire dealers and take up floor space with free tables so that you can get better at the game." You can also test various poker strategies online. If you usually are a tight player, you might experiment online by playing more aggressively than you usually do. Or you might practice bluffing and so on. (Let me add that attempting to bluff is pretty well useless when you're playing for free. Trust me, you will be called.)

As the host of PartyPoker.com, the world's largest online poker site, I invite you to come online and play some poker. You'll be amazed at how enjoyable it is! There are three online poker rooms that host WPT tournaments. PartyPoker.com (www.partypoker .com) sponsors the PartyPoker.com Million. This unique event, the largest on the WPT, is held aboard a luxury cruise ship. UltimateBet (www.ultimatebet.com) is the sponsor of the Aruba Poker Classic in exotic Aruba. PokerStars (www.pokerstars.com) sponsors the PokerStars Caribbean Adventure held at the Atlantis resort in the Bahamas. In addition to these sites, the WPT will be hosting an international gaming site (www.wptonline.com) in the near future where players outside the United States can practice and play poker online.

You Can Get Years of Experience in a Short Time Playing Online

Another advantage of playing poker online is that it is a viable way for you to get experience quickly. You can play any time of the day or night, and you can play for any length of time you want to. If you feel like playing for 20 minutes while you're eating a midnight snack, you can do that; or if you choose to play a tournament that lasts six hours, you can.

For poker players who don't live near a casino, online poker is a savior. Even if you're fortunate enough to have a poker room in your city, playing online can be more convenient than driving to the casino, putting your name on the list, and waiting for your turn to play. As we say on PartyPoker.com, "If you can read your e-mail, you can play online poker."

You Can Win Your Way to a Million Online

The WPT's televised tournaments and online poker have really captured the nation's interest in poker. Prior to the WPT, the perception of poker by most was something that took place in the back of a smoke-filled pool room. Today, poker championships for millions of dollars are taking place in the finest casino properties in the world on a regular basis. Because of that, poker is now viewed as a competition/sport rather than gambling per se. Millions of people have embraced poker and now recognize it as a game of skill rather than pure luck.

Many WPT tournament players earn their buy-ins by playing lower-priced satellites in online casinos. Truly it is beneficial to the poker industry, which is thriving again, for players to try to earn their seats in WPT tournaments by playing online. We've certainly seen the success that online players have had in the great championship events. In the Season 2 WPT Championship tournament at the Bellagio, two players who qualified online made it to the final table. Matt Matros finished in third place and took home $700,000, while Richard Grijalva placed fourth and earned $450,000. Between the two of them, their seats cost only $200! Russian poker ace Kirill Gerasimov won a seat via a satellite in the Season 1 WPT Championship event and wound up taking second place and winning $506,625.

And then there's the famous Chris Moneymaker story. Moneymaker qualified for a seat in the 2003 World Series of Poker in an online satellite that cost him $39—and parlayed it into $2.5 million when he won the title. Moneymaker deserves a lot of recognition for bringing poker to the attention of the public—he is the "Average Joe" who believed in his dream and made it happen. Every small-stakes player in the world looks up to him because he did it. Chris gave hope and incentive to millions of people: "If he can do it, I can do it!" I have a plaque on the wall of my office that says, "Those who achieve SUCCESS are those who take a DREAM and make it come true." Moneymaker certainly did that.

Online poker provides these kinds of opportunities for new players as well as seasoned veterans. At PartyPoker.com, you can parlay a single-table tournament win into a luxurious cruise for two and play to win $1 million in a WPT tournament. For the price of two movie tickets and a box of popcorn, you literally can win a million bucks. Does life get much sweeter than that?

Now let's take a look at some tips that will help you get the most benefit from playing poker online. Translated, that means win as much as you possibly can.

Concentrate on the Game

You must concentrate on the game at hand. When you're playing poker at home on your computer, it's so easy to be watching television, talking with somebody, e-mailing a friend, or eating dinner while you're playing online. But if you want to be successful at online poker, you need to focus solely on the game. You'll find that winners concentrate on the game, while losers scatter their attention among distractions.

Paying attention to the game in cyberspace is just as important as it is when you're playing in a casino. In fact, nothing is more important than observing what's going on in the game—it is the most important prerequisite to becoming a winning poker player.

In online poker, you have the option to play two or more games at the same time. I recommend that you play only one game at a time if you are a new poker player and two games maximum if you're an experienced player. I know some players who play four games simultaneously, and certainly those people are skilled at playing multiple games. Still, I don't believe that you can give each game enough attention so that you don't make mistakes. One screen pops up, another one pops up, a third flashes across the screen, and cards keep whizzing by. Online junkies like the fast-paced action, but I don't recommend it for the vast majority of players.

Play for Free but Not for Long

Just because you've been winning in the free games online, don't expect to be able to jump into a cash game and immediately start winning. In fact, that probably isn't going to happen. You must understand that even though you have won at the play-money tables, you will not automatically win in the real-money games.

Many first-time money players lose their chips when they start playing for hard cash, and they don't know why. One reason is because the training you get at the free tables is not conducive to being successful in real-money games. Let me repeat that—the training you get at the free tables is not conducive to being successful in real-money games. Basically, people play very loose poker in free games. If you were playing a little tighter than your loose opponents in those games, you should have been winning. When you move on to real-money games, you will find that people usually play tighter and more solid poker when they are playing for hard cash.

If you want to become a better player, don't stay in the play-money games for very long because you'll be tempted to play too loose yourself. My recommendation is that you play in free games until you learn how the game is played, understand how the betting works, and have grasped the basic concepts. Then move along to playing in a small buy-in tournament in which your monetary exposure is limited to the amount of the buy-in. (See Chapter 5.)

Recognize That Low-Limit Games Are Action-Oriented

When people are playing for real money, they play more cautiously than they would in the free online games where a lot of newcomers will play any two cards trying to hit *belly-buster straight draws*. Still, games at online sites generally are looser than games in traditional casinos. People seem to gamble more and play faster in cyberspace. Why? Players tend to gamble more when their identities are hidden. It's far more exciting to play a pot than it is to throw your cards away. It's fun to be in the thick of the action.

Most players like to play low-limit poker online. For the most part, there are no ultrahigh-stakes games. Out of over 1,500 "live" games at PartyPoker.com, for example, there are only two tables with $30–$60 limits, nothing higher, plus a reasonable number of $15–$30 games. Most of the games are $3–$6 because those are the limits that most people like to play. Many players tend to gamble more at lower-limit games. Therefore, expect most of the games you play online to be looser than those in traditional casinos that spread somewhat higher-limit games.

USE PROVEN STRATEGIES FOR BEATING FAST, ACTION-PACKED GAMES

Here are a few tips that will help you survive and thrive in the low-limit poker games you play online. For starters, if the table is playing loose, you're better off to be playing tight (and vice versa). You should be selective about the starting hands you play—don't gamble it up just because everyone else is gambling.

Don't play past the flop unless you hit something that you think is the best hand or unless you have a good draw with proper odds. Remember the maxim "fit or fold." If the flop doesn't fit with your cards, fold your hand. I also recommend that in smaller games you play straightforward poker. Don't try to get too fancy by slow-playing your hand or trying to over everybody at the table. Sophisticated plays don't work well in low-limit games.

Don't call your money off. Being a calling station is a surefire way to poverty on the green felt (or cyber felt). It equates to being a loser. And remember, take bluffing out of your arsenal in the lower-limit games. In the vast majority of pots online, the winner will have to show down the best hand.

Realize That Online Play Is Speedy

You are dealt far more hands per hour online than in land-based card rooms. In fact, the speed of online games is two to three times faster than regular poker games. Since no time is wasted with dealers shuffling and dealing, the cards whiz right along.

Online play has fast action and it's exciting. It also rewards you in another way: if you play online tournaments two or three times a day for a few months, you will gain the experience of a player who's been out in the field playing tournaments for five or ten years. Even professional players recognize that dedicated online tournament players can gain as much experience in just a few months as it took the pros years to get. That's the good news.

The bad news is that you're going to take more bad beats playing poker online. I've heard players complain that they're unlucky playing online; some of them have even blamed their losses on the online site. But there's a better explanation than simply bad luck. Since you are dealt at least twice as many hands per hour online as you are dealt in a traditional card room, you're going to take at least twice as many more beats than you do in a land-based casino.

Whether you took a beat because you were unlucky, or whether it was just the natural result of being dealt so many more hands per hour online, you must maintain your composure when you lose a pot—and that means keeping cool twice as often when you're playing online. This is not as easy to do as it sounds.

Recognize that luck is the equalizer, the beauty, and the allure of poker. Luck is always a factor in poker, but the best players will get the money in the long run. Luck is the reason that many people play poker: they believe that if they get lucky, they will win. One of the great things about the game is that anyone can get lucky and win one session or one tournament. Even the greenest player can catch cards and win in competition against the greatest players in the world. Of course, if you sit down across the table from great players 365 days a year, you're probably not going to like your results because, over time, luck is not a factor. In the end, skill prevails in poker.

Play in a Game in Which You're Comfortable

Whether you're playing online or in a traditional casino, you should never play in a game that makes you feel uncomfortable. If you're in a game in which you don't like all the raising that's going on, you should leave it and move to another table. If you're playing in a game in which you're not comfortable with the stakes—they're too high for your *bankroll*, or they're too low for your level of interest, so that you won't play your best—you should not play in it.

Find a game in which you are satisfied with the people you are playing against, and you're comfortable with the stakes you are playing for. If you find yourself losing at one limit, drop down to a lower limit until you start winning again and regain your confidence. Remember, too, that you can always practice or get a refresher course at the play-for-free tables.

It is easy to change tables online. When you play in a traditional casino, there might be only one or two tables of the game and limits that you want to play, whereas online there may be 100 other tables of your game from which to choose. Having a large number of tables in action is an advantage when you want to shop around to find a better game. You're always just a click away from another table.

If you would like to check out all the online action available to you at any given moment, visit www.pokerpulse.com. This site lists the number of people playing in all the online poker rooms and the types of games each site offers.

Wait Before You Click

Don't always use the Advance Action tab even when you know what you're going to do before it's your turn to act. The Advance Action boxes are the little tabs that come up on your computer screen with options such as Bet, Check, Call, Call Any, Fold, Raise, Raise Any, and Raise Pot. In online poker, you have a chance to click one of those buttons before it's your turn to act, whereas in land-based games you don't have that option.

The Advance Action button is a nice feature in that it speeds up play. If a player knows she's going to call, she can click the Call tab and instantly be entered into the pot when the action gets to her. (This action is nullified if someone in front of her raises the pot.) She doesn't have to wait until her turn to make her decision. The same thing applies when she wants to fold or raise. If someone raises in front of you, your Advance Action is no longer in effect. A tab will appear that forces you to wait to act until it's your turn in the betting sequence, just as you must do in a traditional casino.

There are *tells* that you should be aware of in online poker. One of the Advance Action tabs reads "Raise Any." When you're planning to raise the pot no matter what anybody else does, you can click that tab. Be forewarned, however, that when you click the Raise Any button, observant players will recognize that you have a big hand because you didn't take any time in making your decision. This is one of the big tells in online poker. Essentially, your opponents can tell that you have a strong hand because the Advance Action tab lit up instantly, telling them that you intended to raise.

You may not be able to see the whites of your opponents' eyes online, but you can tell something about the strength of their hands by their advanced betting actions. Don't give your actions away— wait until it's your turn to act, especially if you have a big hand.

Schedule Your Online Time Wisely

Budgeting your time is very important when you're playing tournament poker online. You need to know how much time you have to play poker before you sign up for an online tournament. Don't play if you're in a hurry. You can't play in a multitable tournament in which there are 1,000 players if you don't have four to six hours to devote to playing in it. If you only have two hours, you will be tempted to play fast and throw off your money because you need to be somewhere else in a short time. Rather than playing a big-field event, play a single-table tournament that will take only an hour to play if you win it.

If you're on a limited time schedule, you can play a sit-and-go tournament. A sit-and-go event is one in which there is no predetermined starting time. Players sit down at a table one by one, and as soon as the table fills up, the tournament begins. You may be the first player at the table, but as soon as the 10th player comes in, *bang!* The tournament is off and running instantly. (This is how single-table tournaments work, as well as some two- and three-table tournaments.)

In contrast, a multitable tournament is going to have a lot of players in it—and a big prize pool. Multitable events are posted on the site's tournament schedule, and each has a specific starting time. You must register in advance for these tournaments. Suppose you want to enter a $20 buy-in Hold 'Em tournament that begins on Tuesday night at 7:00 p.m. You can register a few days in advance or up to a few minutes prior to the scheduled starting time to play in that event. And you know that if you win that tournament, you'll be sitting there until midnight (and perhaps partying the rest of the night).

Always choose the type of tournament that will best fit your time schedule.

Begin by Playing Small Buy-in Tournaments

As soon as you have mastered the basics in free games online, advance to a small buy-in tournament, preferably a single-table tournament in which you will be playing against nine opponents (when playing Hold 'Em and Omaha). Play in a $5 or $10 buy-in single-table tournament. Once you experience playing for something, you will have a new enthusiasm for the game. I know I've said it before, but here it is again: in poker, decisions should matter. You should be rewarded for good decisions and penalized for bad ones. This concept is critical to your success at playing poker for money.

Try small buy-in tournaments when you first start playing for money. In cash games, you might lose more money than you originally wanted to put at risk. Even in the $3–$6 limit games, which are considered to be pretty small games, it's fairly easy to go through $100. Why not take that $100 and play $5 or $10 buy-in tournaments? That way you can play time and time again on the same bankroll and experience the joy of playing poker for something.

At most sites, single-table tournaments pay three places. Usually, the winner gets 50 percent, second place gets 30 percent, and third place gets 20 percent of the prize pool. (Note that all online poker rooms charge a nominal entry fee, usually about $1, when you sign up to play in a tournament.) If everybody puts up $10 each, for example, the prize pool is $100. The winner at that table receives $50, second place wins $30, and third place receives $20. In other words, you don't have to take first place to make a profit. As you progress in your poker skills, you will start to win some of those tournaments.

Small online tournaments are fun and exciting, and they give you a big bang for your buck. Play one and you'll see what I mean.

Take a Chip Count in Tournaments

You should constantly keep track of everyone's chip count in the tournament. It's easier to do in online casinos than in land-based casinos because the exact amount of chips everybody has is on display right in front of them. In a traditional casino, you have to size up the stacks of your opponents. You are allowed to ask your opponent how many chips he has, and he must tell you, but you usually just estimate his stack size visually. Casinos require you to place all your big-denomination chips in front of your lower-denomination chips because your opponents have the right to know how many chips you have at all times. In online poker tournaments, the graphics are right there on the screen so that you can easily see how many chips the other players have.

Tables are constantly breaking down so that you're frequently moving to a new table in multi-table tournament play. As soon as you get to a new table, look around to see who is the chip leader at the table and which players have more chips than you do. Recognize which players can break you and those who cannot. Automatically program this concept into your mind when you play a tournament, whether online or in a regular casino. This is Tournament 101 basic strategy. Make assessing your opponent's chip stacks something that you automatically do—it is vital to your success.

Have Your Training Aides Handy

A strong advantage to playing online poker is that you can use training aides while you're playing at the computer. You can have books, charts, tables, and notes in front of you to assist you in making decisions, a practice that is totally legal and ethical in online poker. Having instructional paraphernalia handy is especially useful if you are a novice at poker. For example, you can put a starting-hands chart in front of you and refer to it when making a decision about whether to call or fold from a middle position. Be careful, however, not to slow down the game.

If you are an experienced player and have been keeping notes on your usual opponents, you can drag them out and put them by your computer. Maybe you remember the online name of someone who you've played before. Taking a look at your notes, you see that she's a loose player who might raise with any two cards, or maybe she's a solid player who will play certain hands in one situation but not in another one. In a sense, you're "reading" your opponent by reading your notes! Most of the major sites allow you to take notes and keep files on players. You can review your notes by simply placing your mouse over that player at the table and right-clicking it.

Control Your Emotions

Expect to feel every emotion in the book during a session of poker, from the thrill of victory to the agony of defeat. I like what Lyle Berman, a founder of the World Poker Tour and an extraordinarily successful businessman and poker player, said: "In one session of poker, you can experience every possible emotion and learn a lot about a person. You see him during his good times, and you see him during his bad times." He's right. You truly can get to know people by watching them play poker.

You can learn a few things about yourself, too. I know poker players who are quite skillful at poker and should be very successful at the game, yet they don't win at the tables. How can that be? It's because they don't have the right temperament for poker. They get too frustrated with the bad beats and become aggravated. And even when they do win, they're miserable! My advice is this: if poker makes you feel miserable, why play it? If it frustrates you to the point that you slam your fists on the table or bang your head against the wall, maybe poker isn't the game for you.

Make no mistake about it, folks, you're going to face frustration when you play poker. Maybe you couldn't have played a hand more perfectly, yet you still lost the pot. You're going to take bad beats—that's poker! And until you accept them as a part of the natural flow of action in poker, you won't be able to tolerate the emotional swings that you ultimately will have to endure at the poker table.

Tournament poker can be even more frustrating than cash games because when you run out of chips, you're out of the game. In a cash game, you can reach into your back pocket and buy more chips; but when you're playing in a tournament, you can't do that—you're history, you have to wait until the next tournament to get back into action.

Believe me, it can be maddening when you're in a pot in which you couldn't get your money in any better. Suppose you couldn't be in a much better situation—you've got your opponent between a rock and a hard place, and he has to draw to a two-outer with one card to go in order to beat you. All your money is in the pot when *bang!* He hits his dream card, a 20-to-1 shot, and it's bye-bye, birdie for you. It happens—and it's going to happen to *you* when you play poker. I don't care who you are, what stakes you play, or how big a tournament you're playing in—it's going to happen from time to time.

If you can learn to deal with that kind of adversity, poker can make you a stronger person. Poker is about competing with your opponents, as well as—and perhaps even more so—yourself. Remember this: you can't control luck, but you can control how you react to it. If you can tolerate the ups and downs of poker and learn to keep your emotions in check when you suffer a bad beat, it will help you deal a little better with stress in the rest of your life.

The world of poker expands by the day. The most recent innovation is a mobile version of Texas Hold 'Em played on cell phones. This exciting new variation allows you to play against other players for fun and sometimes prizes and also allows you to practice your skills without lugging around a computer. You can learn more about the World Poker Tour Texas Hold 'Em wireless game at www.mforma.com.

Online poker is fun and exciting, but it can also be addictive. Be careful about playing too much and/or losing more than you can afford. Enjoy playing poker, but don't let it rule your life. After all, it is just a game.

Online gaming may not be legal in certain jurisdictions. Make sure to consult with the appropriate authorities in your area before you play for money online.

CHAPTER 9

The World Poker Tour Home Game

Playing a World Poker Tour–style home game is a great way to practice your poker skills. Playing in a home tournament that is structured similar to WPT events can help you learn the ins and outs of the tournament style of poker in an enjoyable and friendly atmosphere. You'll find out from firsthand experience why tournaments are so exciting and so much fun to play.

A home game is just that—a poker game played in someone's home. Friends get together for an evening of fun playing a little poker on the kitchen table. And you can take this to the bank—people are playing poker in home games in every city in the United States every day of the week. Because most poker players do not live near a casino, it is likely that far more of them play in homes than play in casinos.

In fact, most of us learned how to play poker by playing with family and friends in penny-ante home poker games. We humans have a competitive nature, and we like a challenge. We also like to do something enjoyable in our spare time. My friends and I play golf not only for the competitiveness of the game, but also for the social aspect of it—we enjoy the camaraderie we share from spending some time together. People play in home poker games for the same reasons—to enjoy a night out with friends in a competitive atmosphere.

HOW TO SET UP THE GAME

The first step in setting up a home game is to find people to play. With poker so popular these days, that shouldn't be hard to do. It seems that everyone is watching poker on TV and wants to play the Great American Game. Talk to friends, set up a day to play, and invite them over.

To have a successful home game, certain things are a must. Here's a checklist you can follow in setting up an evening of friendly poker action to make sure everything runs as smoothly as possible.

1. Play for stakes that are comfortable for everyone. Since poker is a game that's designed to be played for something, it is important that you play it that way. But that something must be stakes that everybody can afford. Usually, you and your guests will come to a consensus about the stakes you want to play.

2. Set up a start time and a stop time. Never play past the designated stop time. This is vital if you want longevity in your game. A sure way to destroy your weekly or monthly game is to play late. Players tend to lose more than they should when they play overtime, and they are often too tired to go to work the next day. And trust me, folks, playing late does not make your spouse happy.

3. Players should understand that they are expected to play until the stop time. The only two exceptions to this are when a player announces in advance that he or she needs to leave early, or if someone is losing and wants to quit. Note that it is bad protocol for winners to quit before the designated stop time.

4. Play with chips—never use cash. Chips speed up the game considerably. Chips also are the tokens of the trade in casinos, so when you venture from home poker into live casino poker, you'll have some experience handling them. You can play with many types of chips. The pro players use *11.5-gram clay* composite *chips.*

5. Let players know in advance what game(s) will be played. Generally, it is not a good idea to allow players to deal games that haven't been agreed upon in advance. While the WPT features No Limit Texas Hold 'Em, there are a variety of games that you can play, such as stud, Omaha, Razz, and Limit Hold 'Em.

6. Rotate the game to other players' homes or have players chip in to cover the cost of putting on the game—such as food, snacks, and beverages. This is done by charging everyone a fair share of the expenses, or by "cutting the pot" until expenses are covered.

7. Have established rules for things such as misdeals, flashed cards, betting out of turn, and so on. For more information on the rules of poker, Please consult www.worldpokertour.com.

8. Don't allow anyone to criticize players about the way they play. Criticism creates tension. It also will

embarrass players, anger them, or cause them to play worse—and none of those things are good for the game. A festive and fun atmosphere is what people enjoy in home games—and that's what you want to achieve.

A word of caution: it is illegal in many states to have a rake; that is, to make a profit from running a home game or to have money on the table. However, if none of the money goes to the house, it is fine to have a poker night at home. If playing for money makes you uncomfortable, try playing for gift certificates. One of the nice things about playing tournament-style poker is that money is not on the table.

How to Set Up a Home-Game Tournament

Poker tournaments are extremely popular in today's expanding world of poker. One reason players love to play in tournaments is because poker is a competitive sport that requires exercising the brain, rather the body. In addition to skill, the element of luck adds excitement to playing tournament poker. Furthermore, no matter what type of event you play, you get a sense of satisfaction and pride when you do well in a tournament—whether you win a single-table tournament at an online poker room, or do well in a weekly event at a traditional casino, or make it to the final table in a WPT tournament like the pros and amateurs you see on TV.

Practicing your tournament skills around the kitchen table in a home game will help you feel more comfortable and confident when you play in your first poker tournament in a casino or online. You'll understand better how tournament strategy differs from cash-game strategy and how the rising antes and blinds affect the play of the game.

Here are some suggestions for setting up a WPT-style No Limit Texas Hold 'Em home-game tournament.

1. Make the entry fee appropriate and easily afford-able. This is a night of entertainment, so the tournament entry fee could be about the same as the cost of going to the movies, around $20.

2. Set a starting time and emphasize to everyone how important it is to arrive on time. When that time arrives, as casino tournament directors say, "Shuffle up and deal!"

3. Have a random draw for seat assignments. You do this by placing cards facedown on the table, scrambling them, and then letting everyone draw for their seat assignments. For example, if you have 10 players, you would place the ace through the 10 facedown on the table. The player who draws the ace takes Seat 1, the player who draws the deuce takes Seat 2, and so on. If you have 16 players, you will need to have two tables in play. Designate one table as the "spade table" and one as the "heart table." Label a chair at each table as Seat 1. Seat 2 is the next chair to the left of it, Seat 3 is to the left of the second seat, and so on. Place the ace through the 8 in both the spade suit and the heart suit facedown on the table, scramble them, and then allow everyone to draw a seat assignment. For example, the player who draws the five of hearts would go to Seat 5 at the heart table. If you need three or four tables to accommodate everyone, designate a spade table, a heart table, a diamond table, and a club table. Then place the number of cards that matches the number of players facedown for the seat-assignment draw.

4. Everyone starts the tournament with an equal number of chips. The tournament continues until one player wins all the chips in play. When players lose all their chips, they are out of the tournament and must vacate their seats. I suggest that you have someplace where people can go when they *bust* *out*—another card table where they can play gin rummy or backgammon, or even start another poker game. You might even have a DVD of a WPT tournament or the WPT Texas Hold 'Em Plug-n-Play Game playing on your television for your guests to enjoy during their downtime. And, of course, the snack table should always be fully stocked.

5. If you have more than one table in play, keep the tables balanced as best as possible. As players bust out of the tournament and vacate their seats, some tables will have fewer players in action than others. You want to keep the number of players at each table about the same, so you will need to move players when the tables get out of balance. To move a player from one table to another, take the player who is the big blind from the table with the most players at it and move him or her to the most favorable seat at the other table. The most favorable seat will be the one that is farthest from the big blind (not including the small blind or the button). Have a designated "breaking" order of tables. A table gets "broken" when all of the players at that table have been transferred to other tables. For example, the spade table breaks first, the heart table next, and so on.

6. If you allow rebuys—meaning that when players lose all their chips they can buy a new stack and start again—I suggest that you permit only one rebuy per player. Or you might allow players to rebuy during the first "level" of play only and certainly not any longer than during the first two levels. A level is the period of time during which the blinds and the antes remain the same. After the rebuy period has ended, players are out of the tournament if they lose all their chips.

7. If there are 10 players, I recommend paying three places—50 percent for first, 30 percent for second, and 20 percent for third. If there are two tables of players, I recommend paying four places—40 percent for first, 30 percent for second, 20 percent for third, and 10 percent for fourth. Let everyone know at the start of the tournament what the payoff structure will be.

8. Set your *structure*—the levels, the blinds, and the antes—in advance.

THE TOURNAMENT STRUCTURE

All tournaments have structures. Blinds and antes are increased at set times—they must increase in order for a tournament to finish. The longer you want a tournament to last, the longer the time you should allow for each level of play, or the more starting chips you should give to the players. For example, a tournament would last much longer if you played levels of one hour before the blinds went up than if you played 20-minute levels. It also would last longer if everyone started with $2,000 in tournament chips than if they started with $1,000 in chips. Generally, home-game tournaments shouldn't take more than a couple of hours to finish.

Here is my suggested structure for a No Limit Hold 'Em home-game tournament.

1. Start everyone with $1,000 in chips. Although the buy-in is much less than that, recognize that the chips in play are simply tournament chips and don't represent actual dollars. Players like to say, "I raise two thousand!"

2. You will need three different colors of chips. Give players 10 chips of one color (usually red) and designate them as $5 chips; 10 chips of another color (usually green) and designate those as $25 chips;

and seven of another color (usually black) and designate those as $100 chips.

3. For the most part, levels should last for 15 to 20 minutes each. Use a clock or, better yet, a kitchen timer with an alarm on it to indicate when it is time to increase the blinds.

Level	Blinds (SB/BB)
1	$10–$15
2	$15–$25
3	$25–$50
4	$50–$100
5	$100–$200
6	$150–$300
7	$200–$400
8	$300–$600
9	$500–$1,000
10	$800–$1,600
11	$1,000–$2,000

To speed up play as the tournament progresses, you will want to "color up" the chips. Once you get to level three, for example, you won't need the $5 chips any longer. Exchange them by coloring them up to $25 chips. (Exchange five $5 chips for one $25 chip.) When you reach level seven, you won't need the $25 chips any more, so color them up to $100 chips.

MY OWN HOME-GAME EXPERIENCE

I've played in a lot of home games in my life. I love them! Because you know everyone, home games are friendlier and not as intense as casino games. You joke around more in home games. There is a camaraderie and a special bond among poker pals who play regularly in home games that you just don't get when you play in casino games. In short, home games are fun!

I lived in North Carolina for 15 years prior to moving to Las Vegas in 1985. For 8 of those years (from 1977 to 1985), I was a professional poker player playing in home games six nights a week. I even hosted a home game twice a week for a number of years. Playing poker was a true joy back in those days. When one game finished, I couldn't wait until the next day to play again. To this day, some of my best friends in the world are my poker buddies in North Carolina.

Many home games are "dealer's choice": when it's your turn to deal, you can name the game you wish to play. These games can be fun. The problem with them is that some players aren't comfortable playing games they haven't played before, plus you don't get out as many hands when you're always switching games.

When I played in some games back in North Carolina, we had a rule: "If you can explain it, you can deal it." I loved that. Needless to say, we played virtually anything you can think of—wild-card games, every form of high-low split games imaginable, bet-or-get-out games, buy a card and/or replace a card, and so on. We even changed what wins the pot at times. For example, I've played seven-card high-low split with no qualifier for low in which the person who makes an ace-high straight (Broadway) automatically wins the whole pot! In that crazy game, this hand beat all lows as well as flushes, full houses, anything. Make Broadway and scoop-de-do! None of this makes any sense to you? No worries, it was an unusually crazy game!

And if you think that playing wild-card games or different games takes the edge away from a good player, you're wrong. In fact, the more types of poker games you play in your home game, the better it is for good players. That's because they catch on quicker and will know right away which hands are trap hands that they should avoid playing.

A DELIGHTFUL HOME-GAME EXPERIENCE
WITH BEN AFFLECK

Being a commentator on *World Poker Tour* has provided opportunities for me to play in some special home games with celebrities and affluent businessmen. My co-commentator on the WPT, Vince Van Patten, has hosted home games in Hollywood for years and still does occasionally. One of those games was a night to remember.

"Boston Ben" Affleck is a very good poker player who is passionate about the game. He not only played in the $10,000 buy-in No Limit Hold 'Em California State Poker Championship at Commerce Casino in June 2004, he won it! Ben defeated many of the top players in the world to capture that title—worth $356,400 and a $25,000 seat in the WPT Championship at Bellagio in April 2005.

It just so happened that the next night was our weekly home game in Beverly Hills. Boston Ben was the first one to show up. He was beaming from ear to ear, proud as a peacock about his victory. He brought his trophy (and a grocery bag with the cash in it!) with him, plopped it down in the center of the table, and announced, "Boys, you're looking at the California State Poker Champion!" We were all very happy for him and extremely proud of him.

Following the fanfare, congratulations, and hearing about how well he played, it was time to get down to the task at hand—playing some poker. What a night! Every time poor Ben would lose a hand, he got some serious good-natured ribbing. The comments included "I'll be taking that trophy home with me tonight" and "You'd better stick to those tournament players" and "You may be the California State Champion, but you're just a 'chumpion' here." It was a wonderful evening—so many laughs. One of those nights you put in a frame and hang on the wall.

AUTHOR'S NOTE

I've always been a very competitive guy. When we were kids, my buddies and I bet on everything—bowling, golf, even Wiffle Ball—so I grew up gambling. I'm not saying that's a good thing, it just happens to be my background. Danny Robison, the guy who many people consider to be the best seven-card stud player in the world, taught me how to play poker when I was in the seventh grade. Playing cards for money came natural to me since Danny, who was two years older, taught me at such a young age. Although he kept me broke until he left for college, my "training" with Danny paid off for me.

When I graduated from high school, I went to Ohio State on a full athletic scholarship in gymnastics. I played a lot of bridge and poker in college. Bridge is a great game and I love it, but in the bridge world, you just play for the challenge of the game. I soon found that I enjoyed making money at cards more than I enjoyed just playing card games for fun. Naturally, my bridge career tapered off and I eventually became a professional poker player. I've always maintained that when I retire, I want to go back to the bridge

High in the air off the trampoline. This is from when I was a gymnast at Ohio State in the late 60's.

world, but in the meantime, I play poker not only because I enjoy the game so much, but because poker is a game played for money.

Being a commentator on *World Poker Tour* has provided me opportunities to interact with prominent businessmen and Hollywood celebrities. I've played a fair amount of poker with movie star Ben Affleck. In truth, what Ben enjoys about the poker world is that nobody cares who you are—you achieve a reputation in the poker world because of your skill level and your results. Even when you're nominated for an Academy Award (he won one for *Good Will Hunting*), Ben told me, it's subjective and winning is based on somebody's opinion. But when you play tournament poker, nobody's opinion about who the best player is counts—you've proved that you can do it because you're taking home the trophy and the cash. And once you've done it, people acknowledge and respect you as a player.

Affleck knows that if he wins a tournament, nobody has given him anything. He's earned the title and will get respect because of it. That's what happened when he won the $10,000 buy-in No Limit Hold 'Em California State Championship of Poker at Commerce Casino in 2004. Big buy-in tournaments attract many of the greatest players in the world, yet Ben Affleck—an actor—won it. It has always been important to Ben to be recognized as a poker player, not as an actor who plays poker. Certainly, that win cemented his reputation as a "player."

Although Ben has been seen in movies and on television by millions of people, he would be thrilled to win a poker tournament on television. Unfortunately, the big event he won in California for more than $350,000 was not a televised WPT event. The other tournament that Commerce Casino holds, the L.A. Poker Classic, is a WPT televised tournament. Had Ben won that tournament, who knows how many more players would have come into the world of tournament poker? It would have been the most widely watched poker show in the history of television!

Believe me, every single player who plays poker seriously wants to win a World Poker Tour event on television. Your goal is to capture a WPT title. And why not? When you first start playing

I had just won the $10,000 buy-in championship at the World Poker Finals held at Foxwoods in 1992.

tournaments, you're thinking more about making it into the money than about getting to the final table and winning. That's understandable, and it's a good goal in the beginning. But after you make it to the money for the first time, you're going to want more. You get the tantalizing taste of success. "That was really great!" you think. "I want to do it more often. I want to get to the top, I want to win!" And it's going to become somewhat addictive because, deep down, every poker player wants to win a WPT event. Being at a WPT final table on television brings you recognition as a "player," there's no question about it. You're instantly recognized worldwide wherever you go. For the next year or so, everyone's going to say, "Hey, I saw you on that TV show!"

Here's a true story that attests to the popularity of *World Poker Tour*. It was a Friday during the World Series of Poker, and I decided to grab a cheeseburger at the snack bar prior to playing in the upcoming tournament. I sat down next to Beverly Kruskol, a lovely lady and a good poker player from Los Angeles. She began our conversation by saying, "Mike, I really enjoy watching the

World Poker Tour. And you won't believe what happened to me this morning while I was driving to Vegas."

"Tell me about it," I said as I dug into my burger.

"I was stopped by the police," she began.

"Ouch!" I responded sympathetically. "What happened?"

"The officer walked over to my car and said, 'You seem to be in a pretty big hurry. Are you?' "

" 'Yes, as a matter of fact, I am,' " Beverly responded. " 'I'm on my way to play a poker tournament in Las Vegas and it starts at noon.' "

" 'You're a poker player?' the officer asked. "I watch the *World Poker Tour* every week. I love that show."

" 'Me, too,' " Beverly said. " 'And you're going to see me on the WPT one day.' "

" 'Would you tell me with your best poker face exactly how fast you think you were going?' " the officer asked, getting back to the business at hand.

" 'Fifty-five?' " Beverly meekly queried. (Very poor bluff here!)

" 'Well, you're not far off,' " the officer answered. " 'I clocked you at ninety-one miles per hour.' "

" 'Ooops!' " she thought to herself.

" 'Look, I know you're in a hurry to get to your poker tournament, but I have to write you up,' " the officer continued. " 'I'll put you down for going only ten miles per hour over the speed limit, but don't speed the rest of the way.' "

" 'Thanks, I appreciate that. When you see me on the *World Poker Tour*, I want you to tell your friends that you gave me a speeding ticket,' " Beverly said.

" 'I'll be glad to,' " the officer answered. " 'Good luck on making the show!' "

Like Beverly and millions of poker players around the world, if playing at the final table of a WPT tournament is your ultimate poker goal, I sincerely hope that the education you have received from reading this book will help you get there sooner than you ever dreamed possible. Until then,

**"May all your cards be live and
your pots be monsters!"**

GLOSSARY OF POKER TERMS

ace-high A hand that has no special card rankings (no pair, for example) and the highest card is an ace.

aces full A hand with three aces and a pair of any other rank.

aces up A hand that contains two pair: one pair of aces and another pair of any other value.

action A check, bet, call, fold, or raise.

active player A player who is in the pot.

all-in When a player bets all of his or her chips.

all-in over the top Raising with all your chips after an opponent has bet.

ante Amount of money or chips that each player puts into the pot before the cards are dealt.

back into a hand To draw cards that make a hand that is different from the hand you were originally trying to make.

back-door flush draw When you have three cards that would support a flush, but you need the turn and river cards to make a flush.

back-door straight draw When you have three cards that would support a straight, but you need the turn and river cards to make a straight.

bad beat When a lucky hand beats a stronger hand.

bankroll The amount of money that a player possesses to wager for the duration of his or her poker career.

battle of the blinds When everyone folds to the players who have forced bets.

behind When your hand is not the best hand before all the cards have been dealt.

belly-buster straight draw A hand that is missing one card in the middle of a sequence, such as K-Q-?-10-9.

bet To put money in the pot of your own free will; the money you bet.

bet for value When you bet in order to increase the pot size, not to make your opponents fold.

bet the pot To make a bet that is the size of the pot.

bicycle Slang for a straight composed of A-2-3-4-5; also known as a *wheel*.

big blind The forced bet that is made by the person sitting two seats to the left of the button. This is the largest forced bet. In WPT tournament play, this amount increases after each timed round.

big dog An underdog. The player who has a very low chance of winning.

big slick Poker slang for A-K, a very strong starting hand.

blank A card that is not of value to a player's hand.

blind A mandatory bet placed by the two players to the left of the dealer button to ensure action in every hand.

bluff To bet or raise with a weak hand in order to make your opponent think that you have a strong hand.

bottom pair See *top/bottom pair.*

bust a player To eliminate a player from the game by winning all of his or her chips.

bust out To lose all your chips and thus be eliminated from a tournament.

button A white disk that moves clockwise around the table on each hand and indicates where the action begins.

buy-in A minimum amount of money that must be paid in order to play in a tournament or a cash game.

call To match (rather than raise) the previous bet.

cap The number of raises allowed in a game.

catch an inside straight To hit one card in the middle that will give you five cards in sequence.

change gears Strategically alternate your play between conservative and aggressive play.

chase pots To stay in against an apparently stronger hand, usually in the hope of filling a straight or a flush.

check To not bet, reserving the option to call or raise later in the betting round.

check-raise Trapping an opponent by playing weak and then raising over the top of him or her.

a chip and a chair The saying used in tournaments to assure players that anyone can succeed as long as he or she has at least one chip that can be bet to double up.

come over the top To raise or reraise another player's bet.

community cards The cards that are placed faceup on the center of the table and can be used by all of the active players in a hand.

connectors Consecutively ranked cards that can help a player make a straight (K-Q, 9-8, or 6-5, for example).

dead money Money that was put into the pot by players who have since folded.

dealer button The white disk that determines where the dealer starts.

doubling up Doubling your chips by winning an all-in hand.

down cards The cards that are dealt facedown to each player; also known as *hole cards*.

draw To improve your hand so that it beats an opponent who had a better hand than yours prior to the draw.

drawing dead When you cannot win, no matter what cards come up.

early position A position in a round of betting where a player must act before the other players. This is a disadvantaged position.

11-gram clay chips The weight of a WPT or casino-quality clay chip.

fifth street The fifth community card on the table, and the final round of betting; also known as the *river*.

fish A poor player who is losing all of his or her money.

flop The first three cards placed in the center of table that anyone may use to form a hand.

flush Five cards of the same suit.

flush draw When you have four cards of the same suit and need one more card on the turn or the river to complete the flush.

fold To withdraw from the hand and give up your cards rather than continue to bet.

four of a kind Four cards with the same value (J-J-J-J, for example).

fourth street The fourth community card on the table, and the third round of betting; also known as the *turn*.

freeze-out A game or a tournament that is played until one player has all the chips.

full house A hand that contains three of a kind and a pair. (J-J-J-2-2, for example); also known as a full boat.

get full value To raise, bet, or reraise with the intention of getting the maximum pot odds if you win the hand.

good laydown A wise fold in a critical situation.

garfunkel a weak hand

gut-shot straight draw When you are missing one card in the middle of a sequence to make a straight. If you have a 9-8 in your hand and the flop contains a 7-5, you need a 6 on the turn or the river to complete the gut-shot straight draw.

heads-up When the game is down to two players—one on one.

hole cards The two cards dealt facedown to every player at the start of a hand; also known as *down cards*.

jammed pot A pot that has been raised the maximum number of times.

key hand In a tournament, a hand that proves to be a turning point for better or for worse.

kicker The card that is used to break a tie between hands that are similar in value.

late position A position in a round of betting when a player can act after most or all of the other players have acted. This is an advantaged position.

lay down Fold a strong hand in a critical situation.

legitimate hand A strong hand. A hand that is not a bluff.

limping in When a player enters the round by calling, rather than raising, a bet.

live hand A hand that is eligible to win the pot.

long odds When there is a very low probability that something will happen.

loose player An aggressive player who stays in many pots with weak hands.

main pot When a player goes all-in, he or she is eligible to win the main pot. Any bets that are made after that are placed in a *side pot.*

middle suited connectors Two cards in the middle range that connect; for example, 9-8 or 8-7.

monster A hand that has a high probability of winning.

muck To discard a hand. Also, the pile of discarded hands.

No Limit Hold 'Em table stakes At any time, players can bet any or all of their chips.

nut flush The best flush available within each hand.

nut-flush draw When one card will give you the best possible flush.

nuts The best possible hand at the time. Also used as a superlative (for example, "You're the nuts!").

odds The probability of making a hand versus not making a hand.

on a short stack When a player has very few chips.

on the button The best table position in Hold 'Em. The player who acts last in every round of betting.

on the come Continue playing a hand after the flop, in the expectation that one or two cards will come on the turn or the river to make a strong hand.

on tilt Playing recklessly due to frustration.

open card A card that is dealt faceup.

open-end straight draw Four consecutive cards such as Q-J-10-9. In this example, any king or 8 would make a straight.

open pair Two cards of the same rank (value) that are dealt faceup.

out A card that is still in the deck that could improve your hand. A card that could make you a winner.

outdrawn When one person beats his or her opponent by drawing a better hand.

out of position Being at the disadvantage of having to act before your opponent.

outs Cards that will turn the statistical underdog into a winner; also cards that enable a player to win the pot.

over the top Making a large raise.

pair Two cards that have the same value (3-3, for example).

pass When a player folds his or her hand.

pick up the blinds A raise that prompts everyone to fold before the flop.

play fast To bet aggressively on a hand.

playing the board When your best five-card hand is composed of the five cards on the board.

position Where a player sits in relation to the dealer button, which determines his or her betting order.

pot The chips that have been bet.

pot odds The amount of money in the pot versus the amount of money it costs to continue playing.

protect a hand To bet in order to induce other players to fold, thus reducing the risk of having them outdraw you.

put on a hand To guess an opponent's hand and play accordingly.

putting on the heat Betting aggressively to put pressure on the other players.

quads Four of a kind (6-6-6-6, for example).

rabbit hunting Asking to see discards or the undealt part of the deck after the action has been completed.

race When the odds of one hand beating another is roughly 50-50.

ragged flop Flop cards that do not help any player's hand.

raise To make a bet on top of another player's bet.

rank The value of a card or a hand.

reraise To raise on top of a previous raise within the same hand.

river The final community card dealt, which all players may use to form their best hand; also known as *fifth street*.

rock A tight and conservative player.

round of betting The period during which each active player has the opportunity to fold, check, bet, or raise.

rounder A professional player who frequents high-stakes tournaments.

royal flush A hand containing A-K-Q-J-10 in the same suit. The best possible hand in poker.

running bad On a losing streak.

running good On a winning streak.

see To call a bet.

set Three cards of the same rank (Q-Q-Q, for example).

short odds When there is a very high probability that something will happen.

short stack The player with the fewest chips at the table.

showdown After the final round of betting, the players' cards are turned faceup to see who won.

showtunes According to WPT Host Vince Van Patten, what goes off in a player's head when he or she makes an extraordinary hand.

shuffle up and deal Said at the beginning of the WPT tournaments to start action.

side pot A separate pot contested by other players when one player is all-in.

slow-play Play a strong hand as if it's weak.

slow roll Stalling before showing a winning hand in order to frustrate your opponent.

small blind The forced bet that is made by the person sitting one seat to the left of the button. The small blind bet is one-half the size of the big blind.

splashing the pot Throwing your chips into the pot. Considered bad poker etiquette.

stack The number of chips in front of a player.

steaming Playing recklessly after a bad or unlucky hand.

straight Five consecutive cards of mixed suits (9-8-7-6-5, for example).

straight draw A hand that needs specific cards to fulfill a straight.

straight flush Five consecutive cards of the same suit.

structure The schedule by which the antes and blinds (forced bets) increase.

suited connectors Two cards that are consecutive in rank and of the same suit.

super satellite An inexpensive tournament you can enter to win a seat in a WPT main event.

table stakes The limits present at any given table (i.e., 3-6 or no limit) allowing any player to bet all of his chips at any time.

tapis The French term for "all-in."

tell A gesture, expression, or act that gives away the strength of your hand.

tight player A conservative player who bets with strong hands only.

tilt Similar to steaming. Playing recklessly after losing a critical hand.

top/bottom pair The highest or lowest card on the board matched with a card in your hand.

trapping Faking weakness to get your opponent to bet into a strong hand.

trips Three of a kind.

turn The fourth community card dealt, which all players may use to form their best hand; also known as *fourth street*.

under the gun Being in the position just to the left of the big blind.

wheel Slang for an ace-low straight (A-2-3-4-5); also known as a *bicycle*.

wired pair Two hole cards of the same rank.

World Poker Tour (WPT) An annual worldwide series of 16 high-stakes poker tournaments, with buys-ins ranging from $5,000 to $25,000, seen on the Travel Channel every Wednesday night.

World Series of Poker (WSOP) An annual monthlong poker tournament event held at Binion's Horseshoe Casino in Las Vegas since 1949.

WPT Cam A patent-pending camera placed in a poker table that reveals the players' hole cards without anyone else seeing them.

POKER SLANG

Poker players have a colorful way of describing certain hands and situations. For example, two aces in the hole are "American Airlines," or "bullets," or "pocket rockets." In his WPT color commentary, you'll often hear Vince Van Patten call pocket eights "snowmen" or a 10-2 "Doyle Brunson." Here is a list of many of the slang expressions you will hear around the poker table.

American Airlines A-A.

boat A full house.

Brunson 10-2 (the hand Doyle Brunson had in heads-up action both times he won the WSOP).

bullets A-A.

cowboys K-K.

crabs 3-3.

dead man's hand A-A-8-8-X. Named after Wild Bill Hickok, who was shot while holding aces and eights in a five-card draw game.

dime store 5-10.

dog pound K-9.

Dolly Parton 9-5.

ducks deuces (twos).

fishhooks J-J.

good buddy 10-4.

hooks J-J.

Huey, Dewey, and Louie A set of 2s (three deuces).

Jack Benny 3-9 (even in his old age, Benny claimed he was only 39 years old).

Jackson Five J-5.

kicks 6-6.

Kojak K-J.

little slick A-2.

marriage K-Q.

mullets 7-7.

Picasso flop When the flop cards are all face cards (paints).

pocket rockets A-A.

quackers 2-2.

sailboats 4-4.

snowmen 8-8.

spare tire J-4.

speed limit 5-5.

trombones 7-6.

walking sticks 7-7.

Woolworth's 5-10.

RECOMMENDED READING

Poker Books Especially Helpful to New Players

Caro's Fundamental Secrets of Winning Poker, by Mike Caro

No-Limit Texas Hold 'Em (The New Player Series), by Brad Daugherty and Tom McEvoy

Play Poker Like the Pros, by Phil Hellmuth

Internet Texas Hold 'Em, by Matthew Hilger

Winning Low Limit Hold 'Em, by Lee Jones

The Theory of Poker, by David Sklansky

Hold 'Em Poker, by David Sklansky

Poker Tournament Tips from the Pros, by Shane Smith

Books That Will Be Helpful after You Have More Experience Playing Poker

Super System and *Super System II,* by Doyle Brunson

Improve Your Poker, by Bob Ciaffone

Championship No-Limit and Pot-Limit Hold 'Em, by T. J. Cloutier and Tom McEvoy

Championship Tournament Poker, by Tom McEvoy

Championship Satellite Strategy, by Brad Daugherty and Tom McEvoy

Tournament Poker for Advanced Players, by David Sklansky

Hold 'Em Poker for Advanced Players, by David Sklansky and Mason Malmuth

Poker Tournament Strategies, by Sylvester Suzuki

Internet Poker Sites with Good Information

www.cardplayer.com

www.pokerpages.com

www.pokerpulse.com

www.worldpokertour.com

WORLD POKER TOUR
TOURNAMENT PAYOUTS

Casino	Season	Players	Prize Pool	First Prize	Players
Aviation Club de France	1	86	€831,000	€500,000	Christer Johansson—€500,000 Claude Cohen—€160,000 Allen Cunningham—€80,000 Jacques Durand—€32,000 Tony G—€16,000 Alain Hagege—€13,000
Aviation Club de France	2	91	€919,000	€357,000	David Benyamine—€357,200 Jan Boubli—€178,000 Georges Paravoliasakis—€134,000 Jamie Posner—€80,500 Erick Lindgren—€53,600 Lee Salem—€35,700
Aviation Club de France	3	205	€2,050,000	€679,860	Surinder Sunar—€679,860 Tony G—€339,930 Jim Overtman—€203,960 Peter Roche—€135,970 Ben Roberts—€101,980 Dave Colclough—€84,890
Bay 101	1	n/a	n/a	n/a	n/a

Venue		Entries	Prize Pool	First Prize	Payouts
Bay 101	2	243	$1,100,000	$360,000	Phil Gordon—$360,000 Chris Moneymaker—$200,000 Masoud Shojaei—$103,000 Scott Wilson—$79,800 Susan Kim—$68,400 Mark Mache—$57,000
Bellagio	1	146	$1,460,000	$507,140	Gus Hansen—$507,140 John Juanda—$278,240 Kassem Deeb—$139,120 John Hennigan—$83,472 Chris Bigler—$62,604 Scotty Nguyen—$48,692
Bellagio	2	314	$3,044,750	$1,101,980	Paul Phillips—$1,101,980 Dewey Tomko—$552,853 Gus Hansen—$276,426 Abraham Mosseri—$174,585 Tino Lechich—$130,940 Mel Judah—$101,842
Borgata	1	n/a	n/a	n/a	n/a
Borgata	2	235	$1,175,000	$470,000	Noli Francisco—$470,000 Charles Shoten—$235,000 David Oppenheim—$117,500

Casino	Season	Players	Prize Pool	First Prize	Players
Borgata (*cont.*)					Carlos Mortensen—$70,500 Mickey Seagle—$52,875 Randy Burger—$41,125
Borgata	3	302	$3,020,000	$1,117,400	Daniel Negreanu—$1,117,400 David Williams—$573,800 Josh Arieh—$286,900 Chris Tsiprailidis—$181,200 Brandon Moran—$135,900 Phil Ivey—$105,700
Bicycle Casino	1	134	$670,000	$258,000	Chris Karagulleyan—$258,000 Hon Le—$122,550 Stan Goldstein—$61,270 Mark Seif—$38,700 Can Hua—$29,025 Kathy Liebert—$22,575
Bicycle Casino	2	309	$1,546,000	$579,375	Mel Judah—$579,375 Paul Phillips—$293,550 T.J. Cloutier—$146,775 Chip Jett—$100,425 Farzad Bonyadi—$69,525 Phil Laak—$54,075

Bicycle Casino	3	$3,335,000	$1,198,290	Doyle Brunson—$1,198,290 Lee Watkinson—$578,475 Peter Lawson—$272,665 Grant Helling—$170,175 Joe Awada—$132,200 Tom Lee—$99,150
Casinos Spa (discontinued)	1	$234,858	$108,730	Jose Rosenkrantz—$108,730 Jamie Ligator—$45,000 Luis Milanes—$25,120 Dewy Tomko—$14,650 Jamie Anteneloff—$11,510 R. A. Head—$9,420
Commerce	1	$1,360,000	$507,190	Gus Hansen—$507,190 Dan Rentzer—$253,595 Andrew Bloch—$125,460 David Pham—$80,080 Steve Shkolnik—$53,390 Bob Stupak—$46,715
Commerce	2	$3,781,500	$1,399,135	Antonio Esfandiari—$1,399,135 Vinny Vinh—$718,485 Mike Keohan—$359,245 Bill Gazes—$226,890

Casino	Season	Players	Prize Pool	First Prize	Players
Commerce (continued)					Adam Schoenfeld—$170,170 David Benyamine—$132,355
Doyle Brunson NAPC	3	312	$3,026,400	$1,000,000	Carlos Mortensen—$1,000,000 Thang Pham—$496,400 David Pham—$255,000 Erik Seidel—$165,000 Hung La—$120,000 John Juanda—$84,000
Foxwoods	1	89	$890,000	$345,000	Howard Lederer—$320,400 Layne Flack—$186,900 Andrew Bloch—$102,350 Phil Ivey—$75,650 Peter Giordano—$57,850 Ron Rose—$44,500
Foxwoods	2	313	$3,155,000	$1,089,000	Hoyt Corkins—$1,089,000 Mohamed Ibraham—$563,400 Phil Hellmuth—$281,700 Chris Ackerman—$226,925 V. Senthil Kumar—$164,325 Brian Haveson—$117,375
Horseshoe/Gold Strike	1	160	$1,600,000	$589,990	Dave "Devilfish" Ulliott—$589,990 Phil Ivey—$291,030

				Johnny Donaldson—$145,065
				Buddy Williams—$91,620
				Jeremy Tinsey—$68,715
				Tommy Grimes—$53,445
Horseshoe/Gold Strike	2	$3,455,050	$1,278,370	Barry Greenstein—$1,278,370
				Randy Jensen—$656,460
				James Tippen—$328,230
				Chip Reese—$207,304
				Can Kim Hua—$155,477
				Tony Hartman—$120,927
Lucky Chances (discontinued)	1	$456,000	$146,000	Paul Darden—$146,000
				Chris Bigler—$88,000
				Antonio Esfandiari—$44,000
				Phil Hellmuth—$34,000
				Vince Burgio—$26,000
				Tommy Garza—$21,000
Mirage Poker Showdown	3	$2,725,200	$1,024,574	Eli Elezra—$1,024,574
				Lee Watkinson—$513,038
				Gabe Kaplan—$256,519
				John Juanda—$162,012
				Scotty Nguyen—$121,509
				Jim Meehan—$94,507

Casino	Season	Players	Prize Pool	First Prize	Players
PartyPoker	1	177	$1,013,800	$263,850	Howard Lederer—$263,850 Chip Jett—$175,900 Joe "Cowboy" Simpkins—$105,540 Maureen Feduniak—$79,155 Tim Lark—$52,770 Dan Coupal—$43,975
PartyPoker	2	546	$3,847,000	$1,000,000	Erick Lindgren—$1,000,000 Daniel Negreanu—$675,178 Chris Hinchcliffe—$441,463 Steve Zolotow—$259,684 Barry Greenstein—$194,763 Scotty Nguyen—$129,842
PokerStars	1	n/a	n/a	n/a	n/a
PokerStars	2	219	$1,657,498	$455,780	Gus Hansen—$455,780 Hoyt Corkins—$290,065 Daniel Negreanu—$192,270 Michael Benedetto—$132,600 John D'Agostino—$99,450 Remco Schrijvers—$74,590

Reno Hilton	1	$420,746	$168,298	Ron Rose—$168,298 Cal Dykes—$97,772 Tony Le—$50,490 Paul Magriel—$29,452 Mark Edwards—$23,142 T. J. Cloutier—$18,934
Reno Hilton	2	$1,633,700	$604,469	Michael Kinney—$629,469 Paul Clarke—$310,403 Harry Knopp—$155,202 Peter Muller—$98,022 Tony Bloom—$73,517 Young Phan—$57,180
UltimateBet	1	$500,000	Pro—$250,000 Amateur—$50,000	Phil Gordon—$250,000 Juha Helppi—$50,000 Anssi Tuuliverda—$10,400 Kathy Liebert—$8,000 Woody Moore—$6,000 Phil Hellmuth—$30,000
UltimateBet	2	$1,744,000	$500,000	Erick Lindgren—$500,000 Daniel Larson—$300,745 Anthony Fagan—$194,230 Barry Shulman—$112,780

Casino	Season	Players	Prize Pool	First Prize	Players
UltimateBet (*cont.*)					Ted Harrington—$68,920 Rick Casper—$43,860
UltimateBet	3	647	$4,000,000	$1,000,000	Eric Brenes—$1,000,000 Layne Flack—$500,000 Mike Matusow—$250,000 Patrick McMillan—$170,000 John Juanda—$130,000 Vic Fey—$105,000
WPT Championship	1	111	$2,691,750	$1,011,886	Alan Goehring—$1,011,886 Kirill Gerasimov—$506,625 Phil Ivey—$253,313 Doyle Brunson—$159,987 Ted Forrest—$119,990 James Hoeppner—$93,326
WPT Championship	2	343	$8,342,000	$2,728,356	Martin de Knijff—$2,728,356 Hasan Habib—$1,372,223 Matt Matros—$706,903 Richard Grijalva—$457,406 Russell Rosenblum—$322,660 Steve Brecher—$232,862

WPT Invitational	1	104	$200,000	$100,000	Layne Flack—$100,000 Jerry Buss—$40,000 David Chiu—$20,000 Men Nguyen—$10,000 Tony Ma—$7,000 Andy Glazer—$6,000
WPT Invitational	2	196	$200,000	$100,000	Phil Laak—$100,000 Humberto Brenes—$38,000 John Juanda—$18,000 Joe Cassidy—$14,000 Harry Demetriou—$10,000 Antonio Esfandiari—$8,000

n/a = Not applicable, as they were added in Season 2.

WORLD POKER TOUR™

Tournament Schedule*
Season 4

Casino	Location	Dates
The Mirage	Las Vegas, NV	5/22/05-5/26/05
Aviation Club de France	Paris, France	7/25/05-7/29/05
The Bicycle Casino	Los Angeles, CA	8/27/05-8/31/05
Borgata	Atlantic City, NJ	9/11/05-9/16/05
UltimateBet.com	Aruba	9/19/05-9/26/05
Doyle Brunson N.A. Poker Championship	TBD	10/23/05-10/27/05
Foxwoods Resort Casino	Mashantucket, CT	11/12/05-11/17/05
Bellagio	Las Vegas, NV	12/12/05-12/18/05
PokerStars.com	TBD	1/07/06-1/14/06
Gold Strike Casino	Tunica, MS	1/22/06-1/26/06
Commerce Casino	Los Angeles, CA	2/17/06-2/21/06
Bay 101	San Jose, CA	2/27/06-3/03/06
PartyPoker.com	Cruise	3/11/06-3/18/06
Reno Hilton	Reno, NV	3/27/06-3/31/06
Bellagio	Las Vegas, NV	4/04/06-4/28/06

*Dates and Locations subject to change. WPT will film the final table of each event.
 Refer to www.worldpokertour.com for additional info and schedule changes.

FREQUENTLY ASKED QUESTIONS

What is the World Poker Tour (WPT)?
The World Poker Tour is a series of championship poker tournaments that are united under one banner for television. WPT tournaments are aired every Wednesday at 9:00 p.m. ET/PT on the Travel Channel. (Check your local listings for other airings.)

How is a poker tournament different from a regular poker game?
In a poker tournament, players pay an entry fee and receive the same number of starting chips. You play until one person wins all the chips in play. Once a player loses his or her chips, he or she is eliminated from the tournament. In contrast to a regular poker game, a player cannot cash in his chips during the tournament and cannot go back in his pocket, pull out more money, and continue playing when he loses his starting chips. Prizes are paid according to who keeps his or her chips the longest. The player who ends up

with all the chips is declared the winner, but the prize money is paid proportionally to the highest finishers. First place typically earns about a third of the prize pool, and the rest of the purse is divided between the other players who finish in the money (usually about 10 percent of the field).

How does the WPT help television viewers follow the action?

The WPT's innovative technology (the WPT Cam) allows you to see the players down cards while expert commentators allow you to follow and understand the action. Our state-of-the-art technology and on-air graphics let you in on what cards each player is holding. The WPT Cam provides the viewers an opportunity to live vicariously through the players and get a feel for what they're thinking. When a player moves all-in, you know something that his or her opponents do not know—you can see whether he or she is bluffing or actually has the best hand. This adds a dramatic element to the game.

How are tournaments selected to be a part of the WPT?

Already existing tournaments at the finest casinos in the world and top online sites were initially invited to be charter members of the WPT. A few additions have been made since the inaugural season. The tournaments on the WPT are selected based on prestige, prize money, geography, and visual appeal to create an upscale, international image for poker.

Who can enter WPT tournaments?

Anyone can enter. Unlike other professional sports, you don't have to be a pro to play in in a WPT tournament. Part of the appeal of a poker tournament is that as long as you ante up the tournament entry fee, you can compete against the best poker players in the world. You can't play golf on the PGA Tour with Tiger Woods, but you can play poker with the best players in the world by entering a WPT event (and you can win!).

What poker game is played in WPT tournaments?

No Limit Texas Hold 'Em is the poker game played in all WPT tournaments except the PartyPoker.com Million, which features Limit Hold 'Em. In No Limit Texas Hold 'Em, there is no limit on the amount of chips a player can bet at one time, up to the number of chips he or she possesses. In Limit Hold 'Em, there are predetermined limits on the amount of chips he or she can bet at one time.

How many people play poker?

More than 50 million Americans play poker, and there are more than 100 million poker players worldwide. In fact, more people play poker than play golf, billiards, or tennis.

What are satellites?

Satellites are smaller tournaments in which you can win an entry into a larger tournament. The purpose of satellites is to offer players an inexpensive way to earn their entry fee into a much-larger event, such as the championship tournaments on the WPT. Whereas the entry fee into a WPT tournament is $10,000, the entry fee into a WPT satellite may be as little as $200. And for your information, about half the field in every WPT event consists of players who have won their entry via a satellite.

Where can I play a satellite for a WPT tournament?

You can play satellites for WPT tournaments in casinos and at online poker sites. WPT host casinos offer single-table and multiple-table satellites prior to the WPT championship event. Online poker sites post a schedule of satellites you can play to win a seat in an upcoming WPT tournament. It's a way to parlay a small investment into a *large* deposit.

How do you calculate the odds of winning the pot?

Here's an example. Suppose your opponent has two aces and you have an opened straight draw with one card to go. Your hole cards are J–10 and the board is showing 9-8-3-2 in four different suits. You have eight outs (four queens and four 7s) to complete your straight and win the pot. You know 8 cards from the deck, leaving 44 unseen cards. Thus, you calculate that you are about a 5-to-1 underdog to win the pot with one card to go. Therefore, to justify continuing with the hand, the size of the pot should be more than five times the amount it will cost you to call. If the bet on fourth street is $20, but there is $200 in the pot, you should call. If, on the other hand, the pot only contains $50, the correct play would be to fold.

Where can I find more information about the WPT?
Visit www.worldpokertour.com, where you will find the WPT weekly television schedule, a list of upcoming WPT tournaments that you can enter, profiles of WPT final-table players, recaps of past WPT tournaments, a list of WPT satellites, and a glossary of poker terminology. You also will find a description of the casinos and Internet poker rooms that sponsor WPT tournaments, plus a list of WPT products. The WPT store features official WPT merchandise, including tournament poker chip sets, playing cards, video games, DVDs, books, gifts and apparel.

ACKNOWLEDGMENTS

This book was possible because of the commitment of many, especially the dedicated staff of the World Poker Tour. For having the vision that the WPT could work, special thanks go to Steve Lipscomb, Lyle Berman, Audrey Kania, and Robyn Moder. They have been and still are the backbone of the WPT. To my dear friend Linda Johnson, known to many as "the First Lady of Poker," many thanks for your constant support and guidance. And thanks to my many poker-playing friends for providing the stories within. I also owe a debt of gratitude to my WPT partners Vince Van Patten and Shana Hiatt for making all the time on the road enjoyable. They are real pros and truly a delight to work with.

My participation with the WPT has been an amazing ride, filled with terrific experiences and many friends along the way. Special thanks to Steve Lipscomb for including me on the ground floor and inviting me to be a commentator. I credit the WPT for bringing poker to a new dimension. To the joy of everyone in the industry, poker will never be the same again.

I'm honored to be a part of the World Poker Tour and proud of

ACKNOWLEDGMENTS

what the WPT has accomplished. Thanks must be given to members of the WPT staff for helping me to prepare this book: Melissa Feldman, Andrea Green, Andy Ruggles, Katherine Kowal, Chris Lockey, and Elaine Chernov. I would also like to thank the team at Brandgenuity—Andy Topkins, Louis Drogin, Adina Avery-Grossman, Jay Asher, and Cara Lustik—and Matthew Benjamin and the entire HarperCollins team for their efforts in bringing this book to fruition.

And last, but not least, my heartfelt thanks to my editor Dana Smith. Her tireless enthusiasm and guidance were a blessing.

INDEX

.